UNIT 3 (Debates in Contemporary S

SOCIOLOGY PAPER 3 STUDY GUIDE
(with Crime & Deviance Option)

Published independently by Tinderspark Press
© Jonathan Rowe 2021, 2022
www.psychologywizard.net
www.philosophydungeon.weebly.com

Visit the **Sociology Robot** YouTube channel

CONTENTS

SECTION A – GLOBALISATION & THE DIGITAL SOCIAL WORLD

CHAPTER 1 – DEFINITIONS OF GLOBALISATION 7

Problems With Defining Globalisation 8

Defining Globalisation – Exam Practice 18

CHAPTER 2 – DIGITAL COMMUNICATION 19

Relationship to Social Capital 21

Perspectives on Digital Communication 23

Digital Communication: A Toolkit 28

The Digital Revolution 28

The Global Village 29

Networked Global Society 30

Media Convergence 32

Social Media 34

Virtual Communities 35

Digital Forms of Communication – Exam Practice 38

CHAPTER 3 – IMPACT OF DIGITAL 39

Perspectives on Impact 41

Digital Impact: A Toolkit 46

Impact on Culture 46

Impact on Identity 52

Impact on Inequality 57

Impact on Relationships 62

Impact of Digital Communication – Exam Practice 65

CHAPTER 4 – EVALUATION 66

Evaluating Perspectives 70

Section A – Exam Practice 72

Key Research 73

Further Research 75

SECTION B – CRIME & DEVIANCE

CHAPTER 5 – MEASURING CRIME & DEVIANCE 77

Social Order & Control 77

Relativism of Crime 80

Social Construction of Crime 83

Measuring Crime: A Toolkit 86

Official Crime Statistics 87

Victim Surveys 89

Self-Report Studies 91

Measuring Crime – Exam Practice 94

CHAPTER 6 – PATTERNS & TRENDS IN CRIME 95

Perspectives on Patterns & Trends 97

Patterns & Trends: A Toolkit 101

Social Class 101

Gender 103

Ethnicity 105

Age 107

Global Organised Crime 110

Green Crime 112

Patterns & Trends – Exam Practice 116

CHAPTER 7 – EXPLAINING CRIME & DEVIANCE 117

Perspectives on Crime 119

Functionalism 119

Marxism 125

Feminism 130

Interactionism 131

Explaining Crime – Exam Practice 134

CHAPTER 8 – REDUCING CRIME & DEVIANCE 135

Reducing Crime: A Toolkit 137

Right Wing Policies 137

Left Wing Policies 143

Reducing Crime – Exam Practice 151

CHAPTER 9 – EVALUATION 152

Evaluating Perspectives 152

Section B – Exam Practice 161

Key Research 162

Further Research 164

Glossary 166

ABOUT THIS BOOK

This book offers advice for teachers and students approaching OCR A-Level Sociology, **Paper 3 Section A (Globalisation & the Digital Social World)** and **Section B1 (Crime & Deviance)**

The Study Guides for **Papers 1** and **2** will follow.

Paper 3 Section A

This covers a third of **Paper 3** in OCR Sociology. There are 3 questions worth 35 marks out of the 105 marks for the entire paper. It should take candidates 45 minutes to complete.

Paper 3 (Debates in Contemporary Society) reintroduces some foundational concepts that candidates have met earlier in their Sociology A-Level: the idea of **Global Culture**, **Social Control** and **aspects of Identity** along with **Marxism** and **Feminism** from **1A** and also **Postmodernism** that was introduced in **1B**.

Perspectives

This Study Guide reintroduces candidates to 5 important sociological Perspectives: **Marxism, Feminism, Interactionism,** the **New Right** and **Postmodernism**. These were introduced in the Study Guides for Paper 1 but are reiterated here in a new context.

Up until now, Functionalism has appeared as the opposing view to the Conflict Theories (Marxism and Feminism) but it does not appear in **Section A**. Candidates can bring up Functionalist ideas to evaluate Marxism, Feminism and Postmodernism and to help with this I mention them on occasions (however rare such arguments might be in academic Sociology). In **Section B**, Functionalism, the New Right and Interactionism return along with new Perspectives: **Subcultural Theory** and **Left** and **Right Realism**.

Studies

Sociological 'studies' (for A-Level purposes) are often papers published in academic journals, but are sometimes magazine articles, pamphlets produced by charities or activists or popular books. Where texts are particularly famous or influential, I offer their names, but candidates are not expected to know the names of studies in the exam. All the studies referenced in this Study Guide are brought together at the end in a revision aid (p73 and p163).

GLOBALISATION & THE DIGITAL SOCIAL WORLD: CONTENT

What's this topic about?

This introduces you to the main theories in Sociology, in particular the concept of GLOBALISATION and how it influences us. You will also learn about the DIGITAL REVOLUTION (p28) and its IMPACT on society (p39).

This should help you answer some important questions:

- What is globalisation: is it good or bad and (important question) for whom in particular? Is it a powerful force in society or a declining one?

- What are digital forms of communication? How are they different from traditional communication? Who benefits from this new technology and who loses out?

- What are the impacts of digital communication on society? Are our lives enriched or impoverished? Should we be concerned or excited by the prospect of a digitally connected world?

Globalisation

In **1A: Socialisation, Culture & Identity**, you learned about **Global Culture**. Globalisation is the process that is bringing this Global Culture into being – and it is having other effects too.

Globalisation is often described as the world getting smaller. Not physically smaller, of course, but smaller in the sense of being more connected, with faster travel, better communication and stronger economic links. Television brings us news stories from parts of the world that were mysterious to most people in Europe and America only 50 years ago. Air travel means ordinary people can go to faraway places to work or holiday. Migration means that people who used to consider each other 'foreigners' are now neighbours. And of course, the World Wide Web makes communication instantaneous and opens up new knowledge and experiences to ordinary people.

One consequence of this has been the appearance of **Trans-National Corporations** (**TNCs**). These companies started off based in one country but have grown to be worldwide business with more wealth than some small countries. Examples of TNCs include the car company **Toyota** (from Japan), the food company **Nestlé** (from Switzerland) and the fast-food chain **McDonald's** (from the USA) as well as the **'Tech Giants'** like **Facebook** and **Google**.

Alongside the TNCs are other groups with a worldwide reach: **Non-Government Organisations** (**NGOs**) which aren't businesses looking for a profit. These include **Greenpeace**, the **World Wildlife Fund (WWF)** and **Oxfam**. Many of these organisations have the wealth (from donations) and prestige to influence world governments.

CHAPTER 1 – DEFINITIONS OF GLOBALISATION

Globalisation can be understood in different ways and interpreted optimistically (as an exciting new era of opportunity) or pessimistically (as a threat to things that people have valued for generations or a way for the rich and the powerful to exploit everyone on the planet).

Positive Views of Globalisation

The positive view of Globalisation can be summed up in the word '**opportunity**.'

For most of human history, people lived in tribes, cut off from each other, figuring things out for themselves through trial and error, making slow progress and viewing outsiders with suspicion. Globalisation is the end of all that. Now there's one big human tribe emerging with everyone talking to everyone else, learning and progressing.

For some people this is an opportunity to experience new things: to travel, enjoy other cultures and lifestyles, taste new food and listen to new music. It's an opportunity to educate yourself and learn. It's also about political opportunities, for countries that used to squabble over borders to come together and solve problems that would be too big for them alone. Finally, there are economic opportunities, to sell goods to new markets, find new customers and workers, buy new products and offer people services who used to lack access to them. These services can be recreational or lifesaving: everything from video games to vaccines.

Positive views of Globalisation often (but not always) come from the **Postmodernist** Perspective.

Negative Views of Globalisation

Negative views of Globalisation are split between the fear of **homogeneity** and the fear of **exploitation**.

Homogeneity means "everything being the same" and Globalisation threatens to swamp the world with versions of the same cultural products: everyone in jeans and T-shirts, drinking Coke, eating Big Macs, listening to the same R&B music, watching the same TV shows and big budget movies; ultimately, everyone speaking the same language. Quirky local differences and deeply significant religious and cultural traditions all risk being washed away. This means "the world getting smaller" in a less attractive sense: the world getting less interesting and less varied.

Exploitation means the poorer people being oppressed. Critics of Globalisation fear that the only people to benefit from those wonderful opportunities will be the super-rich. Globalisation means that these elite businesspeople no longer have to be restrained by the laws of the country they live in. They are above the law now and can set about making themselves even richer without anything to hold them back. This view of Globalisation focuses on how people in the poorest countries work for a pittance while their resources and environment are stripped away and their own governments can no longer protect them.

Concerns about exploitation often come from the Conflict Perspectives (**Marxism** and **Feminism**).

Problems with Defining Globalisation

Anything with the word 'global' (meaning 'all over the world') in it is going to be huge and complex – perhaps too huge and complex for humans to take it in and sum it up, which is why we have problems defining Globalisation.

Let us use a definition from the sociologist **Anthony Giddens (1990)**:

"[Globalisation is] *the intensification of worldwide social relations which link distant localities in such a way that local happenings are shaped by events occurring many miles away and* vice versa"

This definition includes key features such as: (1) **worldwide social relations**, not just between countries but between continents; (2) **links between distant localities and local happenings**; (3) the '*vice versa*' meaning that globalisation works in two directions, influence coming from far away but also your own influence being felt far away.

But what do we mean by these '*worldwide social relations*'? There are three main definitions.

Anthony Giddens (photo: Eirik Helland Urke)

Cultural Globalisation

This is the way in which cultures that used to be distinct and separated from each other by oceans and deserts and mountain ranges are now encountering each other, blending together and influencing each other. In past centuries, a few travellers, merchants, missionaries and explorers went off to encounter foreign peoples and brought back tales (often exaggerated or garbled) of their culture. Now, thanks to cheap travel, worldwide communication and migration, ordinary people encounter each other's cultures as a part of everyday life.

Sociologists have three responses to this:

Cultural homogeneity: Some sociologists claim this is leading to a **homogenous Global Culture** where everyone acts and things the same, wearing the same fashions, listening to the same music, watching the same films and eating the same food. Marxists are particularly worried that this homogenous Global Culture is really the Capitalist **Consumer Culture** of the USA and Europe, with its inequalities and ruling class ideologies; it is a type of **cultural imperialism**, dominating other societies. **Feminists** are concerned that this culture will not respect the rights of women, exporting sexism all around the world. However, cultural homogeneity might be a *good* thing if it replaces cultural practices that are racist or homophobic or misogynistic (anti-women).

Cultural Defence: Other sociologists point out that communities react to Globalisation by emphasising their own cultural distinctiveness: it becomes *more* important for them, not less, that they teach their children their traditional language and religion and pass on their customs. This can be attractive – such as the struggle to maintain languages like Welsh and Gaelic as Global Culture becomes increasingly anglophone (English-speaking). However, it also leads to **religious fundamentalism**, which (sometimes violently) rejects Global Culture in favour of a hyper-intense version of local religious traditions.

Cultural Defence is covered in more detail in **Chapter 3**, p50.

Cultural Hybridity: Finally, there is the possibility that individuals or groups 'mix & match' the aspects of Global Culture, creating their own **Hybrid Culture** (for a group) or **Hybrid Identity** (for a person). This is a popular view with **Postmodernists**, who claim we construct our identities from the images and ideas available to us in the Media. This choice can be empowering, but there is growing concern about **cultural appropriation**, which is when people from a privileged culture (such as White Americans) adopt aspects of less-privileged cultures in a disrespectful or ignorant way.

US soldier with captured ISIS flag

AO2 ILLUSTRATION: ISLAMIC STATE

Islamic State (also known as **ISIS** or **ISIL**) originated in 1999 but it became famous (or infamous) in 2014 when it captured a big area of territory in Iraq and later Syria. ISIS was identified as a terrorist organisation by the United Nations; it carried out massacres of civilians and the enslavement or execution of prisoners.

ISIS is a religious fundamentalist group and could be interpreted as an example of **cultural defence**. The group rejects 21st century **Global Culture** and wants to go back to the lifestyle and political arrangements of the 7th century CE: the time of the first Caliphate (Islamic empire) after the death of Muhammad. In this 'new Caliphate' many ideas from Global Culture (such as women's equality and tolerance of homosexuality and religious differences) were banned.

Most Muslims reacted with horror to ISIS's atrocities, but some in the Middle East who had experienced invasion by US/UK armies and the collapse of their traditional lifestyles were attracted to its promise to 'turn back the clock.' Because ISIS continued to use 21st century technology, like the Internet and weaponry, it could be seen as a **Hybrid Culture**, mixing ancient and modern ideas.

Because Islamic State tried to set up a country which launched attacks in Europe and Africa, this is also an example of **Political Globalisation**. They stole ancient treasures and oil which they sold on the worldwide black market so **Economic Globalisation** is at work too.

Research: Go back over your notes on **1A: Socialisation, Culture & Identity** and apply these ideas to **Global Culture**, **Consumer Culture**, **National Identities**, **Religion as an agency of social control**, the 'white wannabes' studied by **Nayak** and the debate over 'My Culture is Not Your Prom Dress.'

RESEARCH PROFILE: GIDDENS (1999) - continued

Anthony Giddens's book **Runaway World** *(1999) appears in* **1A: Socialisation, Culture & Identity** *and is expanded upon here. Because of its accessible style and the breadth of topics Giddens addresses, I'd say if an A-Level Sociology student intends to read* **just one book** *by a famous sociologist, it should be this one.*

Giddens identifies Globalisation as a force that changes the way we live, saying: *"We are the first generation to live in global society, whose contours we can as yet only dimly see. It is shaking up our existing ways of life, no matter where we happen to be."*

He discusses how Globalisation causes **de-traditionalisation** – where people question their traditional beliefs about religion, gender roles, etc. People often continue with traditional lifestyles, rather than actually changing them, but their cultures become unstable, because people are aware that there are alternative ways of living; they know that they can abandon their traditions if they want to whereas before Globalisation came along most people found abandoning traditions unthinkable.

When people *do* abandon their traditions, they develop a **'global outlook.'** Giddens calls this emerging global identity **'Cosmopolitanism'** (from the Greek *kosmos* meaning 'the world').

Giddens thinks this leads to **democratisation**: as tradition becomes less influential, people must work out for themselves the role that culture plays in their lives.

This leads to a lifestyle of constant questioning and re-evaluating, which Giddens calls **reflexivity**.

Giddens talks about **manufactured risks** – threats that result from our own runaway technology, like oil spills and nuclear reactor leaks, but also global warming. These risks haven't been around long enough for human beings to judge how big a threat they are or work out what to do about them. They are too big in scale for national governments to tackle singlehandedly. That's why Giddens says there is *"a new riskiness to risk."*

These factors combine to create cultural problems because the decline of tradition, new manufactured risks and constant need to re-evaluate overwhelms us.

Giddens thinks it leads some people to **addictions**, which are attempts to anchor yourself to something stable (the way tradition used to do). The other is **fundamentalism**, as people commit to a single blinkered set of beliefs and ignore (or try to destroy) all the confusing alternatives.

Giddens has a mixture of optimism and caution about Globalisation. However, he rejects the Postmodernist analysis. He claims we are still living in **Late Modernity**, not a new Postmodern society. We do not choose our own identities, instead we rely on **'expert systems'** – therapists, self-help books, online influences, celebrity role models, doctors and scientists. This falls somewhere between the structuralist view that we are controlled by social institutions and the Postmodernist view that we choose our own Identities.

Economic Globalisation

This is the way in which trade, banking and tourism have made different parts of the world depend on each other, creating some staggering inequalities as well as huge profits. This process goes back to the British Empire's creation of colonies in India and Africa and elsewhere. Often, resources (metals, woods, animals, fuels, or just cheap labour) are taken from developing countries to make cheap goods in wealthy countries, while developing countries are sold other products (technology, medicines, entertainment, weaponry) that they would not otherwise produce themselves.

The mixture of examples above (medicines **and** weaponry) shows how difficult it is to agree on this aspect of Globalisation. Are developing countries being helped or exploited, protected or ruined?

Free Trade (Neoliberalism): This is the idea that, if everyone trades freely, everyone benefits. Many developing countries have resources they are not using that the rest of the world needs (minerals or oil underground, forests of valuable timber, fields for crops) and the developed countries have inventions that poor countries would benefit from (medicine, weapons to defend themselves). Why not swap? Critics point out that this trade is stacked in favour of the richer countries and the **Trans-National Corporations (TNCs)** and that poor countries often have their resources taken away (causing environmental damage) and get little back in return.

Protectionism: This is the idea that there should be barriers to free trade to protect local communities. It might mean charging **tariffs** (fees) on things being imported into a country, restricting immigration (especially migrant labour) or the government helping local industries (like factories or farms) so that they can compete with foreign industries that do things cheaper. In 2016, **Donald Trump** was elected US President with the slogan **'America First'** which referred to economic protectionism. This is like an economic version of 'cultural defence' which tries to resist the effects of Globalisation in a country.

Anti-globalisation protest (photo: John Englart)

12

AO2 ILLUSTRATION: THE ANTI-GLOBALISATION MOVEMENT

This is a protest movement that campaigns against Economic Globalisation. In 1999, protesters disrupted the meeting of the **World Trade Organisation (WTO)** in Seattle, USA. 600 were arrested and thousands injured in clashes with the police. The **World Social Forum** was created in 2001 to oppose the activities of groups like the WTO, the World Bank and meetings like the G8 where world leaders gathered to make global economic plans.

The anti-globalists are sometimes termed '**globalutionaries**' (global-revolutionaries) but term themselves the **Global Justice Movement**. They claim that **Neoliberalism** leads to the **destruction of the environment** (e.g. the cutting down of the Amazon Rainforest) and **war** (e.g. the US/UK invasion of Iraq in 2003). They argue these things happen because wealthy people (and TNCs) want the resources (especially oil) in poorer countries and are prepared to destroy the environment and trigger wars in order to get what they want.

However, some anti-globalists are **nationalists** who are concerned that their countries are being changed by immigration and their businesses are being closed down by foreign competition or else bought out by foreign companies. In recent years, many elections and referendums have shown that this protectionist feeling has grown stronger (e.g. the **2016 Brexit referendum**).

RESEARCH PROFILE: ROBINSON (2004)

William Robinson is a **Marxist** who argues a new capitalist class has emerged and a new transnational state exists outside of national borders. The new class are a 'global elite' of businesspeople (they are a "*transnational bourgeoisie*") who have investments all over the world. They are not loyal to any particular country. Instead, they are part of a **transnational state**.

Robinson argues this transnational state and its global ruling class makes up the new 21st century Hegemony. These elites share the same lifestyles and are connected to each other socially. The gap between the rich and poor grows as the super-rich acquire more wealth. They are capable of manipulating or bullying national governments, so 'democracy' no longer means anything

Robinson argues that this Globalised Capitalism is really a world war: "*it is the war of a global rich and powerful minority against the global poor, dispossessed and outcast majority*" (1996).

This idea of a 'war' going on that no one acknowledges is classic **Conflict Theory**. However, Robinson's critics say his theory doesn't explain why wars between nation states continue or why nationalism is growing in popularity. His theory of a transnational bourgeoisie needs more evidence: the existence of super-rich people like **Jeff Bezos** or **Bill Gates** is obvious, but it's not clear they undermine democracy or exploit the poor in the way that Robinson says.

Robinson's view of Globalisation is similar to **Giddens**' view in some ways (e.g. greater **risk**, p10) but he rejects Giddens' idea that Globalisation is making the world more **democratic**; he thinks so-called democracy is an illusion and we are controlled by the transnational bourgeoisie.

Political Globalisation

For most of history, people have organised themselves into tribes, kingdoms or empires. Since the 18th century (the **'European Enlightenment'**), these have been replaced with nation states. Nation states are made up of people with a common history and (usually) language and religion and defined by historic borders. Nation states have a central government that has a responsibility to defend its citizens and secure their wellbeing. **Functionalists** regard the nation state as the best political arrangement for human flourishing and view **National Identity** as important.

Globalisation has brought about **supra-national** ('above the nation') organisations. These are groups like the World Trade Organisation (WTO), the United Nations (UN), the European Union (EU) and the European Court of Human Rights (ECHR).

Supra-nationalism: This is the idea that nation states create many problems (e.g. they fight wars with each other) and are not well equipped to solve modern problems that go beyond their borders (e.g. international crime, global warming). The best solution is for nations to be supervised by larger bodies that impose international laws and make global decisions. Ultimately, such thinking goes, the nation states will fade away and be replaced by larger decision-making bodies – perhaps a single global government.

Nationalism: Nationalists support the nation state as the ideal political settlement, not despite its limitations but because of them: nation states provide freedom and democratic accountability through elections. Nationalists argue that a supra-national decision-making body would in fact be 'an empire' and empires have historically not been very concerned with the wellbeing of their populations. There is a recent surge in **ethno-nationalism**, which is the view that the best nation state is one that corresponds to a single **Ethnic Identity**: this has given support to independence movements in Scotland, Catalonia (Spain) and elsewhere, who argue that even broad national governments like the UK and Spain are not free or democratic enough.

AO2 ILLUSTRATION: THE GREAT FIREWALL OF CHINA

A firewall is a type of computer technology that stops people getting access to a website or database. It's usually to stop hackers getting access to private accounts. The Chinese Communist Party (CCP) has created the 'Great Firewall' stop prevent the population of China gaining access to many foreign websites and cut down on digital information going into or out of China. The point of this is to censor what Chinese people get to learn about. This makes the Great Firewall an example of **Cultural Defence** as well as the use of the Internet to control populations and silence free speech.

The Great Firewall was completed in 2008. It prevents Chinese Internet-users from accessing services like *Google* Search, *Facebook*, *Twitter*, *Wikipedia* (Chinese-language version) and *Amazon*. China has developed its own versions of these services, e.g. *Sina Weibo* (*Twitter*) and *QZone* (*Facebook*). This makes the Great Firewall a type of **Protectionism**.

AO2 ILLUSTRATION: THE EUROPEAN UNION

The **European Union (EU)** came into existence in 1993, formed out of the previous European Economic Community (EEC) of which the UK had been a member. The new EU was **a supra-national body** with its own parliament in which the member nations 'pooled their sovereignty' (i.e. gave up the power to make some decisions so the EU could make decisions for everyone).

The EU is a regulatory body, setting standards and laws for its members. Some of these rules benefit some countries more than others, but the idea was that members would gain more than they lost by pooling sovereignty. In 2012, the EU received the **Nobel Peace Prize** for advancing human rights.

Two EU regulations were particularly controversial. The **single currency (the Euro)** replaced many national currencies in 2002. A national currency (like the British Pound) is a symbol of **National Identity** and the UK did not adopt the Euro. **Free movement of labour** meant that EU workers could travel to any member country and seek work and claim benefits there. This was also seen by some people as a threat to National Identity, especially in the run-up to the **2016 EU (or 'Brexit') Referendum** in which the UK voted to 'Leave' the EU (52% compared to 48% 'Remain').

However, the EU was also supposed to function as a 'counterweight' to American and other global influences. For example, in 2016 the EU established **General Data Protection Regulation (GPDR)** which restricted what companies (including the trans-national 'Tech Giants') could do with private data.

This makes the EU a combination of **supra-nationalism** (since it takes powers from its member nations) and **nationalism** (since it resists the wider effects of Globalisation from outside Europe). The EU allows **free trade** between its member nations but charges tariffs on goods coming into the EU from outside, which is **protectionist** (p12). The culture the EU promotes can sometimes conflict with the culture of its member states, for example Poland's ban on abortion (2021) or Hungary's restricting of homosexuality (2021). By opposing these new laws, the EU is promoting **cultural homogeneity** (p7).

RESEARCH PROFILE: GOODHART (2017)

David Goodhart is a Functionalist who wrote *The Road To Somewhere* (2017) in which he argues that recent politics have been shaped by the presence of two large groups of people in society, which he terms the 'Anywheres' and the 'Somewheres' based on where they feel they live.

The **'Somewheres'** are people with a sense of belonging to a particular place: their home town or country. They tend to live in the countryside or small towns. They are typically less educated and distrust change; they are anxious about immigration and oppose the EU. They make up- about 50% of the UK population.

The **'Anywheres'** are people without this sense of belonging. They would be equally happy living 'anywhere' and don't feel particularly patriotic. They tend to be urban (city-based) and university educated; they are happy with immigration and pro-EU. They make up 20-25% of the population but include a lot of the 'elite' people (top politicians, broadcasters, businesspeople, celebrities) who travel widely and don't have a fixed home for long.

The rest of the population are **'Inbetweeners'** caught between the stay-put mentality of the 'Somewheres' and the footloose mentality of the 'Anywheres.'

Goodhart claims that the views of 'Somewheres' don't get expressed in the Media or in politics, so that (in his view) the **2016 EU Referendum** was a victory for the neglected 'Somewheres.'

Goodhart's views seem to link to the idea of **National Identity** and **cultural defence** (p9) and he presents these values as important to most of the UK population.

Goodhart's critics point out that a lot of UK newspapers support a 'Somewhere' mentality (being patriotic and anti-EU) so this isn't *really* a neglected group. Moreover, a lot of so-called 'Anywheres' *also* have a sense of home and community, but they are equally optimistic about immigration and international cooperation, so there isn't the sort of stark contrast between the two outlooks that Goodhart makes out.

Robinson would link the 'Anywheres' to the transnational bourgeoisie but would reject the idea that the EU Referendum was really a victory for the 'Somewheres' because he doesn't think independent nations like the UK are able to stand up to the transnational state.

Giddens (p10) would link the 'Anywheres' to the new **Cosmopolitan** outlook created by **detraditionalization** and that would suggest their numbers are bound to grow while the 'Somewheres' are going to shrink.

'Challenging and illuminating.' – Will Hutton

THE
ROAD
TO
SOMEWHERE

THE POPULIST REVOLT AND THE FUTURE OF POLITICS

DAVID GOODHART

Conclusions About Globalisation

Defining "*social relations*" as Cultural Globalisation explains a lot of important conflicts going on, such as the promoting of LGBT Pride in countries that had previously tended to be homophobic; it also explains the rise of religious fundamentalism, eating disorders and Internet conspiracy theories as people look for something to replace the sense of tradition that Globalisation has undermined.

However, not everyone experiences these cultural changes equally. Life in big cities is very multicultural, but lots of people live in the countryside or small towns, rather untouched by these changes. This links to **Goodhart**'s idea of the 'Anywheres' and the 'Somewheres' (p16).

Defining Globalisation as Economic explains *why* these changes are happening, especially if you accept **Robinson**'s view of the transnational bourgeoisie manipulating things behind the scenes (p13). People who experience the closure of a business in their community (when it lays off workers, relocates overseas and employs cheaper foreign workers) have a personal experience of this in action.

However, these economic changes don't predict everything and don't account for organisations like the **EU**, which is seen by some Marxists as a neoliberal organisation promoting free trade and Capitalism but viewed by others as an enemy of neoliberalism, promoting the regulation of big businesses and the welfare of workers (p15).

Defining Globalisation as Political links it to some of the big debates of recent years: Do governments have too much power or too little? Should we trust international courts more than our own? Should politicians listen when supra-national organisations like the UN criticise what they do? Was the UK right to leave the EU?

However, lots of people are quite apathetic about these political debates. **Robinson** would argue that national politics is really just a smokescreen to hide the *real* power of the transnational bourgeoisie: elections and referendums don't really change anything.

Other sociologists point out that Globalisation is happening at different speeds in different places: faster in cities than in the countryside, faster in wealthy countries than poor ones; it is resisted by some religious states (e.g. in the Muslim world) and the **Great Firewall of China** is a barrier to some aspects of Globalisation reaching the Chinese people (p14).

Postmodernists claim that Globalisation has transformed society into a new Postmodern form, in which **meta-narratives** have become redundant. This means no one theory can explain anything anymore and Globalisation will mean different things depending on who you are and how you experience it. However, **Giddens** responds that Postmodernity isn't happening; we are living in a **Late Modern** society (p10), and we can still make meaningful theories about things, including the definition of Globalisation.

In **Section B**, you will be able to link Globalisation to the emergence of **global organised crime** (p111) and **green crime** (p113).

EXAM PRACTICE: DEFINING GLOBALISATION

The OCR exam has three questions in **Paper 3 Section A**:

Source A	Source B
Globalisation allows developing countries to catch up with the wealthy industrialised nations through increased manufacturing, economic expansion, and improvements in standards of living. Big companies out-source jobs to developing countries which helps them to grow their economies. By removing barriers to trade, money flows across borders. Globalisation has advanced social justice by focusing attention on human rights worldwide, such as atrocities or the mistreatment of minorities or women, that might have otherwise been ignored.	For better and worse, globalisation has made the world less diverse. Starbucks, Nike and Gap dominate shopping centres all over the world. The sheer size and reach of America have made cultural exchange among nations largely a one-sided affair. Globalisation has created a concentration of wealth and power in the hands of a tiny elite that can gobble up smaller competitors around the globe. Poorer people suffer the disappearance of entire industries to new locations abroad and their politicians are powerless to prevent it.

1. With references to the Source[s], define what sociologists mean by globalisation. **[9 marks: 5 AO1 + 4 AO2]**

*Make two sociological points about globalisation, one based on Source A and one on Source B. You should quote from the source. It's not vital to refer to named sociologists but you should definitely use some sociological terminology. Then offer examples of globalisation and makes sure each example has an explanation of **why** it is globalisation. For example, "Buying junk food because it's sold by transnational corporations that advertise on TV."*

2. With references to the Source[s], to what extent have sociologists successfully defined globalisation? **[10 marks: 4 AO1 + 2 AO2 + 4 AO3]**

Write a paragraph about source A then another about source B. Sum up what's in the source and explain what named sociologists would say about it. Then finish off with a brief evaluation (p66) of each view. Make sure you conclude by answering the question (they have defined it or they haven't or they've partially defined it).

3. Evaluate the view that globalisation cannot be satisfactorily defined. **[16 marks: 4 AO1 + 4 AO2 + 8 AO3]**

*Write three paragraphs. Each paragraph should introduce a sociological idea with some illustration from the real world. Each paragraph should finish off with developed evaluation (see **Chapter 4** for this). For example, you could write about the defining globalisation in cultural terms; then the economic definition, then finish off with the political definition. Don't forget to answer the question: is it possible to define this process of globalisation satisfactorily?*

CHAPTER 2 – DIGITAL COMMUNICATION

This part of the course has the full title **'the relationship between globalisation and digital forms of communication.'**

*The phrase **'digital forms of communication'** is going to be used A LOT and, now that I've introduced it, I shall use the abbreviation **DFOC**. I recommend you do too. Just remember to use the full phrase at the start of an essay to introduce the abbreviation to the Examiner.*

Digital information is information stored in the form of numbers – in effect, computer code. A machine then translates this digital information into something you can make sense of, like an image on a screen or sound from speakers. That's how your mobile phone works.

Older technology uses **analogue** rather than digital information. Analogue means 'representation' (as in the word 'analogy'). Think of a watch where the second hand sweeps round the dial: it is *representing* the passage of time.

Analog is also a word used generally to represent **non-digital communication**. This includes writing things in physical books or letters, printed newspapers and magazines and of course vinyl records.

Vinyl record (photo: Anders Printz)

Think of the advantages of digital music (e.g. mp3 files, songs streamed from Spotify or downloaded from iTunes Store): it doesn't take up any physical space, it cannot be broken or stolen, it's easy to find, it doesn't crackle or hiss, you can manipulate it (such as cutting it up or adding it to a video soundtrack).

Now think of the disadvantages: you can't touch it or look at it, you don't feel as though you own it in the way you own a vinyl record on your shelf, many people feel the sound quality is inferior (it sounds less 'real' than an analogue recording).

The switch to **DFOC (digital forms of communication)** is an important part of Globalisation, because digital information can be sent around the world so much faster and more reliably than analogue recordings.

Positive Views of Digital Forms of Communication

DFOC involves nearly instantaneous transferral of information. The information is broken down into numbers, transferred electronically and reconstructed at the other end. Satellite link-ups mean that the information can be sent all around the world and WiFi means you don't need to be physically connected by a wire or cable to have access to digital information.

Digital information can be copied multiple times with no loss of quality. This means that far more people can all communicate at once, instantaneously, compared to what used to be possible with analogue technology (think of the audience voting on shows like *Strictly Come Dancing*). Digital information can be manipulated (think of what *TikTok* lets you do with a video or how *Photoshop* can alter an image). This ability to manipulate digital information means DFOC is much more interactive than the old analogue sort: if you read a book, the most you can do to interact with it is to write in the margins but if you read a website you can click on hyperlinks taking you to other sites, videos or pop-up captions.

DFOC represents a huge leap forward in human communication, massively increasing the number of people we can communicate with and our ability to interact with them. This ought to be very **empowering** technology for ordinary people.

Negative Views of Digital Forms of Communication

DFOC comes with its own risks, mostly linked to lack of authenticity. The ability to copy digital information creates problems of piracy and fakes. It's much more difficult to assert ownership of digital products, which can be copied and shared millions of times. Digital property can be hacked and digital identities can be stolen. This has led to the problem of unrealistic photoshopped images, 'Fake News' and 'Deep Fake' videos making it hard to tell what's real and what's not.

Critics are concerned that the interactivity involved in DFOC can lead to destructive behaviour. For example, some people maliciously create computer viruses and spread them through DFOC. This is a threat to the privacy and security of ordinary people, but cyber-hacking also threatens national security and is a new type of terrorism and warfare.

Ordinary people behave differently when communicating digitally, leading to problems like online 'Trolls' who threaten and insult strangers or 'Revenge Porn' where jilted lovers upload sexual images of their exes. DFOC makes it very difficult to shield children from violent or pornographic material and means they are not safe from bullying even in their own home.

DFOC adds to the risk of life in the 21st century society, creating more opportunities for crime, antisocial behaviour and confusion. It adds to the stress of modern life, especially for young people, and creates a crisis over what information can be trusted.

Research: Go back over your notes on **1A: Socialisation, Culture & Identity** and apply these ideas to the 77th Brigade of military cyber-warfare; find out about Deep Fakes and Fake News, problems with trolls and the spread of Internet hoaxes and conspiracy theories

Relationship to Social Capital

Social capital refers to the networks of people that enable society to function. 'Capital' normally means 'wealth' so having social capital means having connections that empower you: friends in high places, people with skills that can help you out, favours you can call in, a support group, people who value you and back you up. It includes fame and popularity but also skills like etiquette that enable you to get the best interactions from strangers, such as being able to persuade the police not to arrest you or talk an employer into giving you a job.

Research: Go back over your notes on **1A: Socialisation, Culture & Identity** and apply these ideas to **Bourdieu**'s theory of **cultural capital** and the **Great British Class Survey** which incorporated the idea of social capital into its classifications

DFOC has changed the nature of social capital. You could be very socially isolated person but have lots of online friends and followers. You could have online links to influential or famous people whom you could never meet in real life. Online social capital can help you get jobs, find romance or exert political power, such as campaigning against a celebrity or a company to demand an apology.

Some people can 'monetise' their DFOC, getting earnings through adverts on their channel or endorsing products or brands. This has led to the rise of online influencers.

AO2 ILLUSTRATION: ZOELLA

Zoe Sugg (b. 1990) started a fashion blog when she was 19 that turned into the **Zoella** YouTube channel in 2009, amassing over 10 million subscribers. She films fashion ideas, shopping 'hauls' and vlogs (video blogging) about her daily life as 'Zoella.' In 2013 she was recognised as one of Britain's most influential Tweeters for her Twitter feed and in 2013 she helped launch the **National Citizens Service (NCS)** and became a digital ambassador for the mental health charity Mind. She has since branched out into beauty products, writing books and TV appearances.

Along with her brother (and fellow YouTuber) **Joe Sugg**, Zoe Sugg was nominated as Social Media Superstar at the 2019 Global Awards.

Zoe Sugg is a good example of a young person acquiring huge social capital through DFOC and then monetising that influence into economic capital (she was estimated to be worth over £4 million in 2021).

Zoella (photo: Gage Skidmore)

> **Research:** Go back over your notes on **1A: Socialisation, Culture & Identity** and apply these ideas to **Global Culture** and agencies of **secondary socialisation**; research other online influencers and some of the controversies surrounding them

Not everyone agrees that DFOC increases social capital. You need to be familiar with the Internet's technology, which excludes many older people as well as people who cannot afford the equipment and software needed to promote themselves online or make the time to do it (perhaps, because they have family or working commitments). Online social capital is easily lost once your followers desert you and online celebrities are vulnerable to threats by **'Trolls'** (p60) as well as stalking.

Other critics point out the online social capital comes at the expense of the offline sort: more time spent blogging, tweeting and cultivating your online presence means less time socialising with friends, volunteering for local causes or attending evening classes or live entertainment with other people. **Functionalists** in particular think there is a quality to real-life interactions that is missing online and they worry that online social capital does not bring about social solidarity in the way that engaging with real people does.

RESEARCH PROFILE: PUTNAM (2000)

Robert Putnam wrote **Bowling Alone** (2000) in which he argues that social capital in the USA has been declining since the 1960s. He carries out a lot of statistical analysis on various measures of social engagement: voting, giving blood, going to church, joining community organisations (e.g. local charities, school boards) and sporting leagues – all are going down every year.

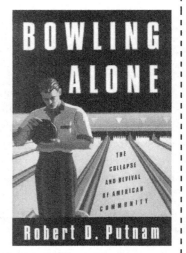

The title of the book comes from the fact that, though more people are going bowling, fewer people take part in organised bowling leagues: they are 'bowling alone.'

Putnam blames this change on several factors, like people moving to the suburbs far away from social venues, the rise in watching TV as a pastime and the generation gap (with young people less inclined to join organisations than their parents and grandparents).

Of course, Putnam can be criticised for only describing the USA. Things might be different in Europe and the UK. However, the biggest criticism is that Putnam ignores the appearance of the Internet. Are people replacing social capital in the offline world with online social capital instead?

Geraci et al. (2018) studies UK Internet-users with fast-speed broadband and concludes that having fast-speed Internet access links to declining participation in social activities, just as Putnam argued was happening in the USA. However, this ignores the possibility that users are replacing their offline social capital with different (and perhaps better) online social capital.

PERSPECTIVES ON DIGITAL COMMUNICATION

Functionalists, who believe in an important biological component to people's social experiences and society's needs, tend to be sceptical of DFOC as a substitute for face-to-face interactions. Other sociological Perspectives look at this new way of interacting differently.

POSTMODERN PERSPECTIVE: POSTMODERNISM

The **Postmodernist** Perspective was introduced in **Paper 1 Section B**. It is a complex set of loosely related ideas originating from the radical ideas of a group of (mainly French) thinkers in the 1960s and '70s. It proposes that the MODERNITY that emerged in the 18th century (the European Enlightenment) is collapsing and being replaced by a new POSTMODERNITY. This Postmodernity is characterised by intense **individualism** and **choice**, the **fragmentation** of old social structures, **diversity** in society and **fluidity** in identities.

Postmodernists see Globalisation as an important driver of Postmodernity: the new **Global Culture** forces everyone to pick and choose how they want to construct their identity and calls traditional lifestyles into question by exposing us to the alternatives out there.

The other driver of Postmodernity is **Media Saturation**: we are bombarded by media images from TV, films, the Internet, etc. and this media overdose changes the way we view reality itself. **Baudrillard (1970)** claims we live now in a confusing **Hyper Reality** where media images are more important than real experiences; **Lyotard (1979)** argues that this state of affairs makes it impossible to believe anything you are presented with is the absolute truth.

Research: Go back over your notes on **1A: Socialisation, Culture & Identity** and remind yourself about **Baudrillard** and then refresh your understanding of Postmodernism from your notes on **Paper 1 Section B**, including **Giddens'** argument that, instead of Postmodernity, we are living in risk-filled Late Modernity.

DFOC appeared in the 1990s and 2000s, long after most Postmodern theories, but they have created *exactly* the sort of conditions that Postmodernists warned were coming.

- DFOC encourages **individualism**, by letting people create their own online identities with groups of friends very different from their offline life
- DFOC encourages **choice** by offering a huge range of products, fashions, ideas and lifestyles – and because DFOC are more interactive, individuals can exercise choices online that they couldn't offline.
- DFOC leads to **fragmentation** as people increasingly live in a social media 'bubble' in contact with like-minded people and lose contact with people who don't share their views
- DFOC leads to more **diverse and fluid identities**, because you can reinvent yourself online as someone new

CONFLICT PERSPECTIVE: MARXISM

Marxism is a Conflict Perspective because it views society as a conflict between the powerless working classes and the ruling class who own all the resources. **Neo-Marxism** has developed this simple idea by suggesting that instead of an identifiable group of rulers (the '**bourgeoisie**') there is a collection of privileged interests in society called **Hegemony**. We have already studied **Robinson**'s idea (p13) that Globalisation has created a new global elite, the **transnational bourgeoisie**, that is waging an economic war against the rest of the human population.

Traditionally, Marxism has been a MATERIALIST philosophy that was concerned about physical wealth (in the form of land, factories and resources like steel and coal) and who controlled these things. From this materialist perspective, DFOC seems rather unimportant: it's just like ordinary communication, only faster and more far-reaching, but the important stuff of people being exploited and the mission to resist Capitalism is going on in the real world.

Intersectionality & Neo-Marxism

Intersectionality is the idea that a person possesses privileged or oppressed identities which can intersect. For example, your White Ethnic Identity confers privileges ("**white privilege**") but your Working Class Identity and your LGBT Sexual Identity intersect with this and cause you to experience victimhood in a more intense way.

Neo-Marxists are in the Marxist tradition of seeing society as in conflict because of Capitalism, but they abandon Marx's strict division of the working and ruling classes in favour of Antonio Gramsci's idea of **hegemonic groups** – groups that want to keep their privileges by keeping other groups down. This enables Neo-Marxists to move beyond issues of class to be concerned about other forms of oppression and marginalisation (e.g. racism, homophobia, transphobia, etc.).

For example, Neo-Marxists have been alerted to how Western societies (i.e. the UK, Europe, America) have a **postcolonial** outlook– they view themselves as superior because they once ruled over other cultures and this sense of superiority is expressed in everyday attitudes. Concerns over **cultural appropriation** and the philosophy behind **#BlackLivesMatter** (see p27) come from this Perspective (as well as others). Neo-Marxists argue that Western society needs to be **de-colonised** by removing the privileges enjoyed by White people and incorporating the voices and perspectives of non-White communities.

This has led to the development of **Social Justice** in politics (p53). Critics complain that it has taken the focus away from the original concern of Marxism: the working class and their struggle against the ruling class.

*A shift from materialist Marxism to a more linguistic focus influenced by Postmodernism has led to **Post-Marxism** (p42) – this is discussed in **Chapter 3**.*

Research: Go back over your notes on **1A: Socialisation, Culture & Identity** refresh your understanding of **Intersectionality**.

CONFLICT PERSPECTIVE: FEMINISM

Feminism is a Conflict Perspective which discerns in society the oppression and subordination (i.e. making them less important) of women by men. The male domination of society is termed Patriarchy and as well as the literal wealth, strength and political power men enjoy this also includes an **ideology** that represents male dominance as 'natural' and which hides and justifies the mistreatment of women.

Feminism has been through at least four 'waves':

- **1st Wave Feminism** in the 19th and early 20th century includes the Suffragettes who campaigned for women to have the right to vote, be educated and inherit property.
- **2nd Wave Feminism** in the 1960s and '70s campaigned for equality in other areas and reforms to society such as the freedom to divorce, access to contraception and abortion and changing attitudes towards sexual harassment and domestic violence. It includes liberal feminists (who want equality with men) and radical feminists (who want to change the way women live in society in a more fundamental way).

These Feminists were MATERIALISTS in a similar way to traditional Marxists: they focused on factors like economic inequality, violence to women, childcare, reproductive rights and women's bodies. From this materialist perspective, DFOC does not seem important: even if women can conduct themselves with freedom online, it doesn't change the material realities of life for women in the real world.

I try to avoid contrasting DFOC with 'the real world' since online experiences are 'real' too. However, I do use 'the real world' when discussing materialist perspectives, because they do regard DFOC as less 'real' than offline material circumstances.

Intersectionality & later Waves of Feminism

Intersectionality originates with **Kimberley Crenshaw**'s *Mapping The Margins* (**1991**) and was quickly adapted by many Feminists. This focus on oppressed or marginalised Identities influenced two more 'waves' of Feminism:

- **3rd Wave Feminism** in the 1990s and 2000s developed an intersectional view of privilege and oppression, with womanhood being one marginalised Identity among others, but intersecting Identities (such as Black women or LGBT women) experiencing oppression that is particularly intense and distinctive.
- **4th Wave Feminism** is often considered to start in 2012 with the launch of Laura Bates' **Everyday Sexism Project (https://everydaysexism.com)** which encouraged women to share their testimonies of sexual harassment and assault. This perspective is linked to Gender Identity Theory.

Intersectionality criticises earlier forms of Feminism as being too concerned with the experiences of White women (perhaps, middle class, able-bodied, straight, White women in particular). This new perspective revitalised Feminism in the 1990s and gave 3rd Wave Feminism a new focus.

3rd Wave Feminism also merges with Neo-Marxism in the **Social Justice** movement, encouraging a shared concern for all sorts of oppressed groups, not just the struggle of women. As with Neo-Marxism, this leads to the criticism that 3rd Wave Feminism is taking its focus away from the original concern of Feminism: women and what unites them, their common experience of subordination to men in a Patriarchal society.

For example, one feature of 3rd Wave Feminism has been a re-think about **prostitution** and **pornography**. Earlier materialist Feminists saw these as social evils and examples of women being exploited by men. Some 3rd Wave Feminists argue that taking part in prostitution or pornography is **empowering** for some women and they argue that it is a judgmental attitude towards sex and the female body that *really* oppresses women. This view is called **sex-positivity** and the sex-positive movement calls for making sex safer, healthier and consensual rather than trying to ban sexual activities. This 3rd Wave view that prostitution should be legalised is opposed by materialist Feminists like **Julie Bindel (2017)** who argue that *"prostitution is inherently abusive, and a cause and a consequence of women's inequality."*

4th Wave Feminism can be hard to distinguish from 3rd Wave Feminism, but the main feature is its focus on the Internet for activism. It has been called *"3rd Wave Feminism with apps"* (**Rod Liddle, 2021**) or *"hashtag Feminism"* (**Jessica Bennett, 2014**, *c.f.* p27).

One of the targets of 4th Wave Feminism is **rape culture** – the idea that ordinary culture is dominated by norms and values that justify male violence and sexual assault on women and this is seen in media images and practices like victim-blaming and 'slut-shaming.'

A shift from materialist Feminism to a more linguistic focus influenced by Postmodernism has led to ***Gender Identity Theory*** *(p54) – this is discussed in* ***Chapter 3***.

> **Research:** Go back over your notes on **1A: Socialisation, Culture & Identity** and update your understanding of **3rd** and **4th Wave Feminism**

Hashtags (photo: nina_pic)

AO2 ILLUSTRATION: HASHTAGS

A hashtag is a word or phrase on social media preceded by the hash symbol (#) that makes a message easy to find. Their use started on Twitter in 2007 but the word hashtag entered the Oxford English Dictionary in 2014.

#EverydaySexism was used by **Laura Bates** in 2012 to encourage women to share their testimonies of being ignored, insulted, harassed or assaulted by men. Within 3 years, 100,000 testimonies had been posted from women all over the world.

In 2013, the hashtag **#KillAllMen** caused controversy when it trended. However, the users were not calling for violence; they were mostly women complaining on social media of being catcalled or sex pestered by men.

In 2017, news broke of multiple accusations of sexual assault against the film maker Harvey Weinstein. The actor **Alyssa Milano** wrote: *"If all the women who have been sexually harassed or assaulted wrote 'Me too' as a status, we might give people a sense of the magnitude of the problem."* Soon, accounts of sexual abuse from women with the hashtag **#MeToo** numbered in the millions.

The hashtag **#BlackLivesMatter** first appeared in 2013, following the acquittal of a US policeman for shooting a Black suspect, **Trayvon Martin**. In the next 5 years it was used 30 million times on Twitter. It trended again in 2020 after the murder of **George Floyd** by a US police officer. The hashtag became a slogan for anti-racism protesters in over 60 countries.

This shows the power of DFOC to draw attention to a cause and how it can spread into offline protests and political action.

#MeToo & #WeTogether (photo: Jeanne Menjoulet)

DIGITAL COMMUNICATION: A TOOLKIT

Digital Forms of Communication (DFOC) include text messages, emails, social media posts, blogs, podcasts, *YouTube* and *TikTok* videos and interactive websites.

Because of the choice and interactivity DFOC offers, this is evidence for the predictions of **Postmodernists** about living in a new age characterised by **media saturation**, **choice** and **fluid identities**. Traditional (**materialist**) **Marxists** and **Feminists** are sceptical about this, pointing out that important inequalities continue to exist in the 'real' world. However, **Neo-Marxists** and **4th Wave Feminists**, who share an **Intersectionality** outlook, think that language itself (**hegemonic discourse**) is the main force that sustains inequality – and these discourses can be revealed and challenged online.

THE DIGITAL REVOLUTION

The **Digital Revolution** has been termed the **Third Industrial Revolution** (after the Agricultural Revolution changed farming and the Industrial Revolution changed manufacturing). It can be dated from **1989**, the year **Tim Berners-Lee** invented the **World Wide Web**.

By the early 2000s, mobile phones and text messaging became commonplace. As of 2020, 67% of the world's population is connected to the Internet. Shopping, banking and even dating have increasingly moved online and, during the **2020 Coronavirus Pandemic**, working and studying from home involved access to the Internet using webcams and live video streaming.

The new DFOC has led to the emergence of New Media, including (1) the **extension of traditional media** like film, TV, newspapers and books through digital formats such as streaming services (e.g. Netflix, BBC iPlayer), apps and e-readers; (2) **new platforms** for media, such as smartphones, tablets and laptops that let people take advantage of the interactive features of DFOC (such as uploading their own videos or maintaining their own social media feed).

AO2 ILLUSTRATION: THE WORLD WIDE WEB

The Internet is a vast number of computers connected together, but the **World Wide Web** is all the web pages that can be found on the Internet. It was invented in 1989 when British scientist **Tim Berners-Lee** developed the systems to enable computers to communicate, in particular URL addresses and HTML coding for creating web pages and HTTP for linking them. Berners-Lee did this to help scientists share research documents, but the Web opened up to the public in 1991.

At first, web pages were quite simple documents with pictures and text – not much different from the pages of magazines but with hyperlinks connecting them. From 2004, **Web 2.0** developed. This new version of the Web is much more interactive and allows users to post up their own content without needing to know computer programming languages. This has led to the rise of social media and the big 'Tech Giants' like **Google**, **Facebook** and **Twitter**.

RESEARCH PROFILE: CORNFORD & ROBINS (1999)

Is the Digital Revolution really a 'revolution'? **Cornford & Robins (1999)** argue that the New Media are **evolutionary**, rather than **revolutionary**. In other words, they are a progression from what already existed, but not a brand-new experience. Interactivity was present in traditional media, such as the letters pages in newspapers, or phoning in to radio or TV programmes. They argue that DFOC have made this interaction faster and easier but that is all.

Cornford & Robins also argue that DFOC will not revolutionise society either. The same sort of Capitalists control the New Media as controlled the old media. They are only concerned with making a profit and they use the New Media to spread **ruling class ideology** and **manufacture consent** to the Capitalist system. The 'choice' and 'interactivity' offered through DFOC is largely an illusion or confined to trivial matters, not important matters of wealth and power.

Cornford & Robins are coming from a traditional (**materialist**) **Marxist** Perspective (p24) – hence their scepticism about the Digital Revolution. Notice the publication date (1999) is from *before* Web2.0 and you could argue this makes their criticisms out-of-date because they only apply to the less-interactive world of the first **World Wide Web** (p28).

Research: technologies that contributed to the Digital Revolution (dial-up modems, broadband, smartphones, 5G, etc.)

THE GLOBAL VILLAGE

The **Global Village** is a phrase that puts across the link between Globalisation and the Digital Revolution: DFOC has 'shrunk the world' to make it like living in a village. In village life, everyone can know who everyone else is; they can communicate easily, share problems, work together on projects. They also share the same disasters and are equally affected by antisocial behaviour. No one is anonymous or uninvolved.

DFOC has created this Global Village by putting people in touch with (potentially) every other person on the planet. As with village life, we are able to share problems and get help (such as working together on climate control or applying for jobs in other countries).

We are also exposed to each other's problems, such as the rise on international terrorism and crime made possible by DFOC. This links to the idea of **manufactured risk (Giddens,** p10).

The concept of a Global Village also links to Giddens' ideas of **de-traditionalisation** and **cosmopolitanism** (p10) and the conflict detected by Goodhart between **'Somewheres' and 'Anywheres'** (p16).

AO2 ILLUSTRATION: ZHU LING'S MYSTERY ILLNESS

In 1995, **Zhu Ling**, a young science student at Beijing University, fell mysteriously ill. Doctors were unable to treat her and, as her condition worsened, her friends appealed for help on the Web (this was before the **Great Firewall** existed, p14). Over 1500 responses flooded in from around the world and a third correctly diagnosed thallotoxicosis, a rare condition caused by exposure to the element **Thallium**. Zhu Ling was treated using advice from doctors in many countries and made a partial recovery. The mystery of how and why Zhu Ling was poisoned with Thallium is still unsolved but this was a milestone case in 'remote diagnosis' by DFOC and an example of the Global Village at its best.

RESEARCH PROFILE: McLUHAN (1964)

The term 'Global Village' was coined by the Canadian commentator **Marshall McLuhan** in the 1960s, a long time before the **Digital Revolution** itself. McLuhan was farsighted in seeing where **Globalisation** was heading even without DFOC. McLuhan argues that due to communication technology *"the whole civilized world is made the psychological equivalent of a primitive tribe."* He suggests that this will bring about the **end of individualism** – whereas Postmodernists usually claim DFOC intensify individualism.

McLuhan ponders the good and bad sides of this. He argues that the Global Village is *"fission, not fusion"* – in other words, we will experience all this conflicts, rivalries and feuds of village life but on a global scale, rather than happy and harmonious integration.

McLuhan also famously stated ***"the medium is the message."*** This means that the qualities of a medium have as much effect as the information it communicates. For example, reading a description of an event in a newspaper has a different effect from hearing about it, or seeing a picture of it, or watching a video.

*The idea that 'the medium is the message' is useful to criticise **Cornford & Robins** (p29) because it suggests the interactive DFOC of Web2.0 will affect people differently from the old-fashioned electronic communications they were discussing. It will also be useful when we look at the **Impact of Digital Communication** (p39).*

NETWORKED GLOBAL SOCIETY

Social networks are another term for **social capital** (p21): they are the links you have to other people who can provide you with information, resources, financial or emotional support. Social networks include your friendship groups, your work colleagues, your family and people you know through hobbies, pastimes, clubs, political organisations or religion. **'Networking'** has become a word for increasing the usefulness of your social network.

As well as personal networks, there are now Digital Social Networks of contacts online. This has created a **Networked Global Society** on a worldwide scale, thanks to the **World Wide Web** (p28) and DFOC. These networks can be more powerful than the local networks of people you know personally and meet face-to-face. For example, if you are looking for a job you might ask family, friends and neighbours – your local network. But if you have a global network, people might tell you about job opportunities in other countries.

Most networks are **horizontal**, putting you in touch with people connected to you for different reasons (e.g. ex-girlfriends, former co-workers, old schoolfriends, people who share your memes). **Vertical networks** are people linked by a particular interest, like taste in music, career, age or hobby. Vertical networks include **ResearchGate** (a network for academics and researchers) or **Mumsnet** (for women and parents, p54). Since 2020, vertical network sites having been gaining members and horizontal network sites have been losing them. The advantage of vertical networks is that they filter out material that is irrelevant to you (holiday photos, pictures of cats, out-of-date memes) or opinions you don't like.

*Vertical networks will be important later on when you study **Impacts of Digital Communication** (p39) and debates around social media bubbles and echo chambers.*

AO2 ILLUSTRATION: LINKEDIN

LinkedIn is a networking site launched in 2002. It is rather more vertical than sites like *Facebook* or *Twitter*, because it's a professional network site to help people find jobs or recruit new employees. The focus is on sharing your work-related achievements and your LinkedIn profile functions as a CV, advertising your career history, qualifications and testimonials.

As of 2021, *LinkedIn* has over 750 million members from 200 countries. However, because it is an all-purpose professional network site, it is less vertical than *Goodwall*, which is specifically for people at the start of their careers looking for opportunities.

Research: other networking sites and how they are used: try Behance and StackOverflow as well as ResearchGate, Goodwall, Goodreads, BlogHer, Dribbble, Letterboxd, Mumsnet and others.

RESEARCH PROFILE: CASTELLS (2000)

Manuel Castells is a (former) Marxist sociologist who wrote *The Information Age* (a trilogy of books, concluding in **2000**). Castells argues that a new kind of Capitalism that he calls '**Global Informational Capitalism**' (or '*Informationalism*') has emerged. This new Capitalism has shifted away from directly controlling oil, gas, coal or the factories that use them in favour of controlling information through global networks.

These networks are global in scale and very fluid: they bring together experts to complete a project then disperse them, rather than maintaining a workforce with a wage. Ordinary people, with little mobility, education or special skills, are excluded from these networks.

Castells argues we now live in an **Information Age** which can *"unleash the power of the mind"* and lead to more productivity, more leisure and less waste of resources if it can be managed properly (which involves challenging Global Informational Capitalism, which only cares about its own power and profits).

This network of elite Capitalists resembles the **transnational bourgeoisie** described by **Robinson** (p13). It is similar to the argument by **Cornford & Robins** (p29) that the arrival of DFOC has not changed the essential nature of Capitalism, because the Capitalist ruling class has adapted to it and uses it to maintain their own privilege and exclude everyone else. Castell's idea of the new Information Age has similarities to **Postmodernism**'s claim that society has entered a new phase.

MEDIA CONVERGENCE

Media convergence is the way different kinds of media that originally had their own distinctive platforms now come combined on a single platform.

For example, people used to get their radio broadcasts through a radio, their TV through a television set, their print news through a newspaper and their novels through books, while going to a cinema to see the latest films and listening to music on vinyl records.

Nowadays, all of these media can be accessed through apps on a tablet or smartphone: TV and radio can be streamed through apps like BBC iPlayer, most newspapers have subscription apps and there are new online news services, books can be read (or listened to) through e-reader apps like Kindle and music can be streamed through services like Spotify.

This means that when people access one type of media, they tend to get the whole converged package that goes with it. This creates **cultural convergence**; the emergence of a **Global Culture** based around Western (European and North American) TV, film, music and sport. This supports the Capitalist system that creates this technology, because you need to own these expensive smartphones and computers to access the media products.

AO2 ILLUSTRATION: AMAZON

Amazon started out as an online shopping website, founded by **Jeff Bezos** out of his garage in Seattle, USA. It began as an online bookstore in 1995. The website soon moved to sell more than just books and in 2007 *Amazon* release the **Kindle** e-reader. By 2010, customers were buying more e-books than physical books from *Amazon*.

In 2011, *Amazon Video* started selling and renting digital film and TV shows. In 2014, the *Echo* became the latest example of media convergence, being a device that can respond to voice commands (through its AI named '*Alexa*') to access music, audiobooks, podcasts and websites as well as operate other linked technology, such as the *Amazon Prime* TV channels. Since 2015, *Amazon* has produced its own films and TV series.

Amazon is a powerful example of **media convergence**, but has been criticised for driving out smaller competitors, destroying High Street shopping and treating its van drivers and warehouse workers poorly. Its success has made Jeff Bezos the richest person in the world (worth $200 billion in 2021).

Research: go back over your notes from **1A: Socialisation, Culture & Identity** and link these ideas to the Amazon workplace and secondary socialisation

RESEARCH PROFILE: BOYLE (2007)

Raymond Boyle (**2007**) argues that media like television has changed from being **supply-led** to being **demand-led** because of the **interactivity** in DFOC. For example, we are no longer limited by TV schedules. We can 'binge watch' entire series and options like 'the red button' let viewers construct their own viewing experience. Because of streaming services, viewers can watch shows at times that suit them and catch-up services let them access shows they would otherwise have missed.

All these media services can now be accessed through a single device, like a Smart TV, tablet or smartphone. Media is more interactive, allowing viewers to schedule their own entertainment with 'watchlists' and 'favourites' and media providers offer suggestions based on previous viewing.

This focus on the **choice** provided by media convergence links with a **Postmodernist** view. However, the tendency of media providers to offer more of what you've already seen can end up limiting your choice, which is an example of the risk pointed out by **Giddens** (p10).

*Notice the dates of Boyle's research: he's talking about the effect of **Web2.0** (p28) and doesn't suffer from being out-of-date like **Cornford & Robins** (p29).*

SOCIAL MEDIA

Digital Social Networks in the early years of the **World Wide Web** (p28) allowed users to post up comments and replies on bulletin boards on web pages. Since the arrival of **Web2.0**, users can upload their own multimedia content (images, videos, etc.) creating **Social Media**. This includes fully interactive services like Facebook, Instagram and Twitter.

Individuals use Social Media to stay in touch with family and friends and their wider community. Businesses use social media to market their products to customers. There is a lot of overlap between the two, especially as the interactivity of DFOC allows customers to leave comments and feedback on products or individuals to promote themselves like a business (for example, selling their helpful A-Level Study Guides).

Because of the **Networked Global Society** (p30), the reach of Social Media goes far beyond your home town or country. This means families can stay in touch around the world and businesses can market their products in other countries. It also means terrorists and criminals can plan their crimes on a much wider scale.

Because of **Media Convergence** (p32), Social Media tends to overlap with offline life: people upload phots of their meals or interrupt conversations to check updates. This blurring of the distinction between the online and offline links to **Postmodernist** ideas about **media saturation** and **Hyper Reality** (p23).

AO2 ILLUSTRATION: TWITTER AND TWITTER-STORMS

Twitter is a Social Media service that was launched in 2006. Users can post short (140 character) messages and links which form long threads of conversation, often identified by **hashtags** (p27). In 2020, there were 186 million *Twitter* users, with the most popular accounts (in terms of followers) being former US President Barack Obama and pop stars Katy Perry and Justin Bieber.

*The fact that 38 million Twitter users are American and the top accounts are all American celebrities reveals the US-bias in **Global Networked Society**.*

Twitter is used by many politicians, journalists and businesses to reach the public in a more direct way than ordinary press statements or adverts. It is also used by activists and protestors trying to draw attention to their causes. A **Twitter-storm** is a spike in posts around a particular topic or hashtag, usually taking the form of complaints and arguments. These 'storms' often make it into national news and cause politicians to change policies, public figures to issue apologies or businesses to drop clients. A **'pile-on'** is when lots of Internet-users get involved in such a storm, heaping criticism on one particular user for their views.

Twitter is often called upon to **regulate** Tweets that are hateful or deceitful (p40). In 2021, US President **Donald Trump** was banned from *Twitter*, for inciting violence and making false allegations of voter fraud. However, a lot of abusive behaviour continues unchecked on *Twitter* – *c.f.* **Trolls & Incels** (p60).

RESEARCH PROFILE: RONSON (2015)

Jon Ronson's book *So You've Been Publicly Shamed* (2015) studies Twitter-storms and public shaming. Ronson reflects on his own experience of shaming a 'spambot' account that was copying his Tweets and interviews others who were at the centre of Twitter-storms, either as instigators (e.g. a woman who showed co-workers making sexist jokes and this led to one of them being sacked and then the woman losing her job too) or victims of these online outrages. The target of the public shaming is at the centre of an online 'pile-on' which can include abuse and threats, even death threats and (for women) rape threats.

Ronson argues that public shaming has a long history, especially in the USA. It was phased out as a punishment as ruining a person's reputation was increasingly seen as cruel. However, Ronson argues that DFOC has led to *"a great renaissance in public shaming."* The idea that online behaviour serves a social function – and one that is very old but in a new form – is a **Functionalist** insight. **Feminists** and **Marxists** argue that public shaming is an effective way for ordinary or marginalised people to call very powerful and privileged people to account in a way that would not be possible otherwise. **Postmodernists** view the volatile nature of DFOC as part of the fragmented nature of postmodernity.

Bor & Peterson (2021) explain this behaviour with the Functionalist **Mismatch Hypothesis**: mismatches between DFOC and human psychology mean that relationships become dysfunctional without face-to-face meetings

VIRTUAL COMMUNITIES

A Virtual Community is a **Digital Social Network** where the users interact online but do not interact (and perhaps do not even know each other) offline. This can include organised groups on **Social Media** (like Facebook groups) but the best examples include websites that offer users a virtual environment in which they can create online identities (called **avatars**). These avatars can be completely different from the user's offline identity.

Increasingly, animated graphics or **virtual reality** (**VR**) technology makes participating in a virtual community as socially complex as physical interactions offline. Avatars offer users anonymity or the chance to act out very different social roles.

Virtual Communities can also be text-based. For example, *Facebook* groups can be private and have moderators ('Mods') who control who is or isn't allowed to join the discussion. These groups are often based around lifestyles, hobbies, political persuasions or religion.

AO2 ILLUSTRATION: MMORPGs and WORLD OF WARCRAFT

A MMORPG is a **Massive Multi-Player Online Roleplaying Game**. These are virtual communities where users create avatars inspired by fantasy or science fiction and to explore or compete in a virtual world – often one with monsters to overcome and treasure to capture, giving a loose objective to the social experience.

The most popular MMORPG is **World of Warcraft (WoW)** which was launched in 2004 and in 2020 there were 4.9 million players. Players create fantasy characters and explore the world of Azeroth, interacting with other players or computer-controlled characters.

Players join together in groups called 'guilds' but the guild members might know nothing about each other's offline lives. Players also meet on online forums (a type of **Social Media**) to share their experiences and post up fan art, fiction and videos.

People marry each other's avatars inside the game and conducted online romantic relationships. 16% of male players and 5% of females reported physically dating someone they met in a MMORPG (**Yee, 2006**).

In 2020, after a scandal involving sexual abuse in the company that created *WoW*, there was an in-game protest conducted by the players' avatars who staged a 'virtual sit-in' outside a tavern in Oribos (a fantasy city in the virtual game world).

World of Warcraft has spilled over into TV advertising, books, cartoons and a 2016 movie, which is an example of **media convergence**.

RESEARCH PROFILE: NOVECK et al. (2021)

The 2020-22 Covid Pandemic has increased the importance of virtual communities, according to research led by **Beth Simone Noveck**, who carried out interviews with 50 leaders of *Facebook* Groups in 17 countries, along with 26 global experts in online community building. The researchers also ran a YouGov survey of 15,000 Internet users in 15 countries.

77% of respondents indicated that the most important group they're a part of now operates online.

Noveck concludes that DFOC connects people with like-minded people but also facilitates hate groups and dangerous movements. It enables isolated users to feel less alone, leading to strong bonds. There was a link between online communities and meet-ups offline. The Covid Pandemic intensified digital social networks, as people haven't been able to get out and meet with friends and family as they normally would.

Noveck's research is a good example of TRIANGULATION using multiple research methods.

Conclusions About Globalisation & Digital Forms of Communication

The **Digital Revolution** (p28) hasn't just changed the way a bunch of scientists and university students share research – it has gone on to connect the world in new and unexpected ways and become the powerful engine of Globalisation.

A **Networked Global Society** (p30) has come into existence, putting the majority of the world's population in instant contact with each other. This new **Global Village** (p29) has far-reaching consequences.

One consequence is that ordinary people greatly increase their **social capital** (p21). Anyone can start amassing *Facebook* friends or *Twitter* followers or start sharing their self-made videos on *YouTube* or *TikTok* and some people have become 'influencers' and media stars by doing this. For other people, these **digital social networks** provide company, emotional support, advice and entertainment.

However, the group that has benefited most from these developments is the group that was already wealthy and powerful to start with. Big businesses have grown bigger, becoming world-straddling **Trans National Corporations (TNCs)** and the big **Tech Companies** have a level of control over our daily lives – for example, to invade our privacy or cut us off from communicating by banning us from their platforms – that goes beyond anything most governments can do.

Marxists have identified the emergence of a new class of global super-rich who are beyond the power of any individual country to control or punish. Most of them make huge profits through using the Internet to their advantage.

Some countries and communities are disturbed by these changes. Digital forms of communication make it very difficult to keep secrets, to control who people speak to or what they see. They open up huge opportunities for criminals and terrorists to carry out their plans on a worldwide scale. They allow deranged and dangerous people who would otherwise be lonely misfits to discover each other and grow more extreme.

One response to this is **cultural defence**, usually in the form of censorship. The **Great Firewall of China** (p14) is one example of a state making sure that Globalisation only happens at the speed and in the way that it decides is best – even though this ignores its citizens' basic freedoms to communicate and learn about the world outside.

Religious fundamentalism is another response which involves trying to 'turn back the clock' and live in the world as it was before Globalisation – perhaps *centuries* before Globalisation.

Even in countries that offer more freedom, people experience anxiety about these developments. Many parents try to limit their children's 'screen time' or use parental settings to limit children's access to adult websites or gambling sites. **Twitter-storms** (p34) erupt and politicians have to respond quickly to the public mood; this is sometimes good for democracy but it can also create a dangerous 'mob mentality' online. Furthermore, the digital network makes it possible to engage in 'cyber-warfare' – such as fears that a country's enemies are interfering with its elections by spreading propaganda and 'fake news' online.

EXAM PRACTICE: DIGITAL FORMS OF COMMUNICATION

The OCR exam has three questions in **Paper 3 Section A**:

Source A	Source B
During the Covid Pandemic, I don't know what I would have done without my online community. Being able to log in and make contact with friendly people, know that they were experiencing the stress and isolation of lockdown, it made all the difference to my mental health. Friends I used to meet in person for a coffee I could now meet online, using Zoom. We moved our weekly pub quiz onto Discord. Lots of Facebook friends became true friends. I feel my social circle has grown as a result and made me stronger too.	Online friends aren't real friends. People chase after 'followers' and 'likes' but the click of a button doesn't show real engagement or concern. The person who cares about you is the person who will drive you to the hospital or house-sit for your dogs. No amount of faceless thumbs-up or heart emojis online adds up to a single meaningful friendship. Anyone logging on looking to feel more connected to other people is chasing an illusion. Your real community is outside your front door: your neighbours.

1. With references to the Source[s], define what sociologists mean by digital social networks. **[9 marks: 5 AO1 + 4 AO2]**

*Make two sociological points about digital networks, one based on Source A and one on Source B. You should quote from the source. It's not vital to refer to named sociologists but you should definitely use some sociological terminology. Then offer examples of networks and make sure each example has an explanation of **why** it is a digital network. For example, "Twitter because you can follow celebrities online and interact with them."*

2. With references to the Source[s], to what extent are digital social networks explained by Postmodernism? **[10 marks: 4 AO1 + 2 AO2 + 4 AO3]**

Write a paragraph about source A then another about source B. Sum up what's in the source and explain what named sociologists would say about it. Then finish off with a brief evaluation (p66) of each view. Make sure you conclude by answering the question (Postmodernism does explain these networks or it doesn't – or perhaps it is just a partial explanation).

3. Evaluate the view that digital forms of communication are becoming more significant in the global world. **[16 marks: 4 AO1 + 4 AO2 + 8 AO3]**

*Write three paragraphs. Each paragraph should introduce a sociological idea with some illustration from the real world. Each paragraph should finish off with developed evaluation (see **Chapter 4** for this). For example, you could write about the Global Village, Media Convergence and a Networked Global Society. Don't forget to answer the question: are digital communications becoming more important or not?*

CHAPTER 4 – IMPACT OF DIGITAL

Digital Forms of Communication (DFOC) have the potential to transform our society – but do they? The 'impact' of DFOC includes changes, for better or worse, in our identities, social inequality and our relationships.

Positive Views of Digital Impact

This is a NEOPHILIAC viewpoint: it sees the **New Media** and DFOC as beneficial for society.

The **Digital Revolution** (p28) has led to a huge increase in **choice**: where you buy your products from, how to pay for things, where to get your news from, what fashions or celebrities to follow, what groups to join and how to interact with people.

Neophiliacs think this choice is **good for the economy**, creating new online business (e-commerce) and new technologies. It is also **good for democracy**. It is easier for people to educate themselves about important matters and play an active role in debate and decision-making, through online petitions or taking part in **Twitter-storms** (p34). The Internet can give a voice to people who previously didn't get heard and it can hold politicians to account by exposing their mistakes and failings. It allows like-minded people to join together and organise protests.

Postmodernists tend to be neophiliacs, although some are aware of the uncertainty and risk involved in the Digital Revolution. **Post-Marxists** (p42) and **4th Wave Feminists** (p25) are neophiles who believe in the power of DFOC to resist Capitalism and challenge privilege.

Negative Views of Digital Impact

This is a CULTURAL PESSIMIST viewpoint. Cultural pessimists believe that the benefits of the **Digital Revolution** have been exaggerated by neophiliacs.

Some cultural pessimists point out that DFOC isn't really something new. Accessing the Internet still requires TV screens, phone lines, etc. People have always signed petitions, written letters of complaint or contributed to the letters pages of newspapers. The only new thing about DFOC is its speed – it offers immediate and constantly changing information, news and entertainment.

A different sort of cultural pessimism argues that the increased choice and interactivity has led to a decline in the quality of **Popular Culture**. There might be more channels for viewers to choose from, but this has led to a dumbing down of content (e.g. endless repeats, reality TV and gambling). This view is particularly associated with **Functionalists** who view DFOC as less authentic than traditional interactions.

Cultural Pessimists also criticise the **polarisation** of online debate – the way DFOC encourages people to adopt extreme positions and not listen to opposing viewpoints, often surrounding themselves with **'echo chambers'** which are digital social networks where everyone you are connected to shares the same opinions as you. They link this to the **Culture Wars** (p46), **Twitter-storms** (p34) and the rise of toxic subcultures like **Incels** (p60).

Regulation of the Internet

The World Wide Web was created by inventors and businesses who were **neophiliacs**, excited about the idea of **free speech** and **free information**. However, many **cultural pessimists** now insist that the Internet is in need of regulation. Even neophiliacs acknowledge that it is easy access to pornography online and free speech is often used to express homophobic, transphobic and racist views and even support violent terrorism.

Regulation would mean setting limits on what can be said or shown online. But what should those limits be and who should police them? One view is that the **'Big Tech' companies** themselves should regulate the Internet. For a long time, the Tech Companies resisted this idea, but they have started taking down offensive material and banning users who post hate speech. For example, since 2017 *Twitter* has been taking down posts that *"harass, intimidate, or use fear to silence another person's voice"* – including the account of former US President Donald Trump.

Another argument is that **state governments** should regulate the Internet and use the law to punish people who incite hate or terror online. Governments have started moving in this direction, which also alarms libertarians who don't want to see free speech become a crime.

Libertarians argue this is unjustified **censorship of free speech**. They are also concerned that regulators are not unbiased and censor some views but not others. However, libertarians tend to be Functionalists or traditional (materialist) Marxists and Feminists; many other groups feel that censorship doesn't go far enough (*c.f.* **Trolls & Incels**, p60). Libertarians illustrate their position by quoting the historian **S.G. Tallentyre** (**1906**): *"I disapprove of what you say, but I will defend to the death your right to say it."* In other words, even hateful and violent things should be allowed to be said and not restricted.

RESEARCH PROFILE: CURRAN & SEATON (1991)

James Curran & Jean Seaton argue that patterns of ownership reveal how the news media operate. Capitalism tends to concentrate ownership in fewer and fewer hands and this is happening with the news. This leads to a narrowing of the range of opinions in the news media and a decline in quality and creativity as the Media keeps recycling the most popular things.

Ideally, the news media would reflect the interests of an audience (otherwise they go out business) and it would be easy for anyone to report news themselves on **Social Media**. However, this doesn't happen, because powerful news media companies are perceived as telling 'the truth' rather than just an opinion. **Neophiles** hoped the Internet would bring more points of view into the news media, but Curran & Seaton believe that big news organisations have successfully defended their control: they are an **oligarchy** (a small ruling group). Curran & Seaton point out that national governments limit what news is reported, so state-run news companies (like the BBC) don't offer different views either.

Curran & Seaton believe that the Internet does not represent a break with the past and it does not offer a new environment for ordinary people and marginalised voices to be heard.

PERSPECTIVES ON IMPACT

When it comes to the impact of **Digital Forms of Communication** (**DFOC**) there are a lot of splits within the sociological Perspectives that normally seem to have such united fronts. The good news for students is that this gives you a lot to write about when evaluating different positions.

POSTMODERN PERSPECTIVE: POSTMODERNISM

You would expect **Postmodernists** to be enthusiastic **neophiles** (p39) who view the impact of DFOC as being entirely beneficial. After all, DFOC offers **choice** in a world of **media saturation** and **diversity**. The ability to take on a different identity online links to **fluidity**. Even the multiplying conspiracy theories, Internet hoaxes and fake news online ties in with **Lyotard**'s idea of '**the death of Meta-Narratives**' because there is no longer one 'truth' that everyone accepts.

However, some Postmodernists point out the problems with the uncertainty and confusion this produces. **Zygmunt Bauman (2013)** argues that *"uncertainty is here to stay"* and that in the 21st century each of us needs to *"develop an art of living permanently with uncertainty."* For many people, the pressure to make choices and live without a 'meta-narrative' they believe to be absolutely true creates a stressful sense of uncertainty: are we making the right choices? what is the point of it all? **Lyotard (1979)** calls this state of uncertainty *"the postmodern condition"* and **Bauman** claims we just have to get used to uncertainty as best we can because it's here to stay.

Another troubling idea comes from **Michel Foucault (1926-1984)**, which is that anything that claims to be true is really just a type of language called **discourse**: a sort of 'loaded' way of speaking that society treats as significant and authoritative. Foucault argues that even scientific language is just a discourse: it's only 'true' because society has decided to privilege certain scientists, the things that they say and the way that they say them.

RESEARCH PROFILE: FOUCAULT (1966)

Michel Foucault argues that power is expressed in language and power determines what counts as true and what does not. Foucault argues that *"power is everywhere"* and *"comes from everywhere"* but there are *"regimes of truth"* which means that some language is respected but other language is not. Language affects the way we view the world and causes us to accept things as 'true' or 'false.' Different **discourses** are always battling in society, but none of them is objectively true. Foucault argues that, if you want to change power in society, you need to **deconstruct** the **dominant discourses** that support the *status quo*: show them up for being contradictory or absurd and make them seem unbelievable to people. He calls this '**problematising**' – pointing out the problems with taken-for-granted ideas – and writes:

"Discourse transmits and produces power; it reinforces it, but also undermines and exposes it, renders it fragile and makes it possible to thwart."

41

Michel Foucault (1926-1984)

It's worth spending a bit longer on Foucault's theory. He imagines society as dominated by ideas coded into language itself. Just by accepting these **discourses** 'at face value' you buy into the ideas in them. Examples including laughing at racist jokes, accepting sexist stereotypes, dismissing some ideas out-of-hand as 'impractical' or 'extremist.' To break free of these limiting forces, you have to **deconstruct** language – expose the faults and contradictions, question everything, turn ideas on their heads and show that things are **problematic**.

Foucault was *not* a Marxist. He recognised that dominant discourses and regimes of truth tended to support dominant groups in society, but he didn't think the dominant groups *deliberately* created these discourses to back up their privileges. He saw it as a two-way process, with language shifting to benefit the dominant groups and groups becoming dominant because of the discourses that support them (think of how the Queen's face on stamps and banknotes supports the British monarchy, but the Queen didn't personally arrange for it to be there).

The Conflict Perspectives have taken aspects of Foucault's theory, creating what has been termed '**Applied Postmodernism**.'

CONFLICT PERSPECTIVE: MARXISM

Foucault's ideas about **discourses** and **deconstruction** don't appeal to traditional (materialist) **Marxists**, who view power as coming from control over **the means of production**, not language. Marxists have a related concept called **ideology** which is different from Foucault's discourse because ideology is an outright lie being presented as truth (e.g. that the ruling classes are doing things in everyone's best interest) whereas Foucault argues 'truth' is only *whatever discourse happens to have the most power at any given time*.

Despite this difference, some **Neo-Marxists** in the 1980s adopted Foucault's ideas and created **Post-Marxism**. Post-Marxists argue that, since society is dominated by a Hegemony (a group of powerful interests that **manufactures consent** through the Media), then most language will be **hegemonic discourse** – language that backs up hegemonic privileges. Post-Marxists see it as their mission to **deconstruct hegemonic discourse** and destroy its power by showing it up for what it is. This leads to a policy of policing language and 'calling out' hegemonic discourse (for example, people sharing racist jokes or using stereotypes about the poor or using words like 'cripple' to refer to people with disabilities).

It suggests that decolonising Western culture means questioning linguistic uses of 'white' and 'black' (e.g. giving someone a 'black mark') and deconstructing popular TV shows, films and everyday behaviours – such as the bias in school curriculums that focus on European history, geography and literature.

Post-Marxists believe that bringing about changes in the way people use language will bring about changes in the way people view society – ultimately, it will lead to people rejecting Capitalism and inequality. **Materialist Marxists** are sceptical about whether meaningful change can happen by focusing on language rather than changing material realities like money and work.

The difference between **Post-Marxism** and **Postmodernism** is that Foucault thought it was impossible to know the truth about reality, but he urged people to deconstruct dominant discourses in a spirit of playful mischief. Post-Marxists use deconstruction more seriously to undermine Capitalism; this is why it can be considered **'Applied Postmodernism.'**

RESEARCH PROFILE: LACLAU & MOUFFE (1985)

Ernesto Laclau & Chantal Mouffe developed Post-Marxism with their book *Hegemony & Socialist Strategy* **(1985)**. They reject some very traditional Marxist ideas, like everything in society boiling down to the conflict between the working class and ruling class and defining power as control of the economic means of production. They also reject the idea that Capitalism must inevitably collapse. These ideas are essential to traditional (Materialist) Marxism, so rejecting them is a major break with the past.

Laclau & Mouffe focus instead on **hegemony**: the way privileged people in society are motivated to keep things the way they are and persuade everyone else to go along with them. Instead of focusing entirely on **social class**, they look at how people can be marginalised (denied privileges) because of their race, ethnicity, sexuality or other **aspects of Identity**. They suggest that marginalised people need a discourse that enables them to **resist hegemonic control** and articulate their oppressed situation.

Laclau & Mouffe argue that Post-Marxists need to focus on **'antagonism'** (a point of conflict) to mobilise people – antagonisms could include the environment, LGBT rights or antiracism instead of the working class vs ruling class antagonism. Post-Marxists claim there is a need to challenge dominant discourses about these ideas and develop new discourses that demand **social change**.

CONFLICT PERSPECTIVE: FEMINISM

Foucault's ideas about **discourses** and **deconstruction** don't appeal to traditional (materialist) Feminists either. 2nd Wave Feminists were well aware of sexist language and assumptions, but they focused on winning economic and biological equality for women, rather than trying to redefine things. They recognised **gender roles** as a **social construct** that oppressed women but they saw these roles as being passed on through **socialisation** and **social control**, not language.

3rd Wave Feminists in the 1990s started incorporating Foucault's ideas, starting with **Queer Theory**. Queer Theory focuses on gender behaviour that doesn't fit into the binary of masculine/feminine, such as Gay Subcultures, Drag Subcultures and Trans Identities. This **deconstructs gender discourses**, showing that there are lots of other ways of living and behaving outside of the **dominant discourse** of masculine/feminine.

4th Wave Feminists goes further than this, proposing **gender fluidity**: there are dozens, perhaps hundreds, of Gender Identities on a spectrum and a person might change from one to another. Even biological sex, which was assumed in the past to be a binary (male/female) is reinterpreted as a spectrum and a Trans person might change their sex that was assigned at birth rather than just changing their Gender Identity.

4th Wave Feminists believe that bringing about changes in the way people use language will bring about changes in the way people view sex and gender — it undermines the discourse that gives power to males/masculine and marginalises other sexes and genders; this is why it can be considered '**Applied Postmodernism.**'

These ideas can be termed **Gender Identity Theory**: gender is each individual's lived experience and is a spectrum, not a binary. There are dozens of genders, not just two (some say 57, 63 or 100). As well as masculine and feminine, there is transmasculine, transfeminine, genderqueer, demigirl, demiboy, agender, androgyne, neutrois, pangender, polygender and many more.

Some Gender Identity Theorists go further, arguing that sex itself is a social construct. According to this view, people are **assigned** a binary sex at birth (male or female) but, in reality, sex is no different from Gender Identity and your Gender Identity might turn out to be different from your assigned sex. This idea is essential to current campaigns for the rights of Trans people.

As with Marxism, this argument owes a lot to the influence of Postmodernism, especially Lyotard's idea that no scientific theory can be objectively true or account for the experiences of everyone. Instead, people are radically individual and subjective.

Gender Identity Theory has led to conflicts between Materialist Feminists (who oppose the idea of gender but believe in biological womanhood) and 3rd and 4th Wave Feminists (who embrace the idea of multiple genders as essential to Identity). Materialist Feminists sometimes term themselves **Gender Critical Feminists**, but their critics call them **TERFs (Trans-Excluding Radical Feminists)** and accuse their views of being Hate Speech. This battle plays out online, especially on the *Mumsnet* website (p54).

RESEARCH PROFILE: BUTLER (1990)

Judith Butler is a LGBT activist and **Feminist** who wrote the deeply influential book *Gender Trouble* **(1990)**. Butler focuses on how both gender *and* sex are socially constructed – an idea that was still controversial among 3rd Wave Feminists but has become much more accepted among **4th Wave Feminists**.

Butler argues that 'woman' is not a category of people but is **performative**. Womanhood is not something you *are*, it is something you *do*. By **performing** gendered behaviour (e.g. in the way we dress or work) or gendered speech (the way we talk), we construct a **gendered reality** around ourselves.

Judith Butler (photo: Andrew Rusk)

This is similar to **Foucault's idea of discourses** but it includes physical behaviour as well as language and imagery.

Butler recommends **deconstructing hegemonic gender performances**, for example by focusing on **'queer'** appearance and behaviour that doesn't fit in the standard categories. Butler singles out **Drag Subculture** as something that makes audiences realise that sex is fluid and gender is a performance. Butler views the standard categories of male/masculine and female/feminine as oppressive and sees queerness as something that liberates people.

4th Wave Feminists use **deconstruction** to undermine the **dominant discourse** about sex and gender. However, **Materialist Feminists** are sceptical about whether any meaningful change can happen by focusing on language rather than changing material realities for women, like money, the law and work (i.e. Patriarchy in offline society). They also criticise 4th Wave Feminism (and **Judith Butler**) for abandoning a strictly biological definition of 'woman.'

Research: go back over your notes from **1A: Socialisation, Culture & Identity** and update ideas about **Gender Identity** in the light of these theories

*The debate within feminism over gender gets pretty intense and sometimes turns hostile, especially online. See the article on **Mumsnet** for more details (p54).*

DIGITAL IMPACT: A TOOLKIT

The OCR Specification asks candidates to reflect on the impact (both positive and negative) of **Digital Forms of Communication** (**DFOC**) and to do so in a global context.

IMPACT ON CULTURE: CONFLICT & CHANGE

Postmodernists argue that Global Culture has come into existence and is going through rapid changes. Change is stressful for people. **Bauman (2013)** argues that people have to live with **uncertainty** now (p41); even though he is not a Postmodernist, **Giddens (1999)** argues that people experience **de-traditionalisation** and have to live with **manufactured risk** (p10).

AO2 ILLUSTRATION: THE CULTURE WARS & 'WOKE'

The **Culture Wars** refers to a conflict across society, but particularly one that plays out in the Media and through DFOC, between two broad groups of people:

Progressives are optimistic about change, uninterested in tradition (including National Identity), opposed to religion and supportive of **Conflict Perspectives** generally. They likely voted against Brexit, wholeheartedly support LGBT rights and oppose racism; in the USA they support abortion but oppose gun ownership. They often support the removal of statues or images that cause offence and generally support **Social Justice** (the reordering of society to give power to previously marginalised groups and remove privileges from dominant groups, p53).

Traditionalists are pessimistic about change but see value in tradition (including National Identity); they see the positive side in religion and are more likely to be religious. They support the **Functionalist** Perspective generally. They likely voted for Brexit, they are cautious in their support for LGBT and antiracism and might oppose these movements; in the USA they are anti-abortion but pro-gun. They are offended by the removal of historic statues and images and alert to the destructive side of the **Social Justice** Movement.

The two sides in this 'war' have trouble sympathising with each other. Online progressives are often given the sarcastic name '**Social Justice Warriors**' (or **SJWs**). They are also identified as '**woke**' (because they are 'awake' to the problems in society and the need for change). Online traditionalists are sometimes called '**Neocons**' (because of a political philosophy called Neoconservatism which supports similar causes). They are also accused of being part of the '**Alt-Right**' which is a US-based online movement that supports nationalism and racism.

It is claimed **Digital Social Networks** produce 'bubbles' or '**echo chambers**' where people only encounter like-minded views which leads to polarisation (getting more extreme and inflexible). '**Cancel Culture**' is where people are silenced during **Twitter-storms** (p34), by **Trolling** (p60) or the closing of venues to prevent them speaking. Online complaints can lead to people being banned from **Social Media** (p40) or even losing their jobs. However, critics claim that concerns about the rise of Cancel Culture is just a **moral panic** aimed at discrediting **Social Justice**.

RESEARCH PROFILE: DUFFY (2021)

Bobby Duffy, director of the Policy Institute, conducted a survey of 2834 UK adults in 2020, weighting the results by age, gender, ethnicity, class, education and family type. He discovered there are not two 'tribes' in the Culture Wars, but rather four:

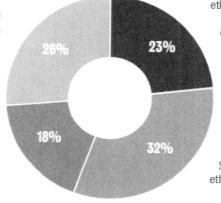

Traditionalists
Oldest and most heavily male group. Most nostalgic for country's past and proud of British empire. 97% think political correctness gone too far, and most likely to feel UK has done enough on equal rights for historically marginalised groups.

Progressives
Youngest group, with highest education level. Most likely to think women's rights, ethnic minority rights and trans rights not gone far enough. Most likely to be ashamed of British empire, and most in favour of political correctness.

The Disengaged
Stand out for neutrality on politics and Brexit. Least likely to take a position on equal rights for women and ethnic minorities, and least likely to take stance on culture war issues.

Moderates
Support greater rights for women and ethnic minorities – but less strongly than Progressives. Agree political correctness gone too far, yet not nostalgic for past nor proud of empire.

Image: The Policy Institute

The Traditionalists are the only group with a male majority (61%) and the only group opposed to the **Black Lives Matter** movement. Progressives are the youngest group, the most ethnically diverse and over half have university degrees.

Although Moderates are the largest group, online they are 'drowned out' by the more active Progressives/Traditionalists. Which way Moderates shift will have a big effect on society.

Duffy & Hewlett (2021) propose that the Culture Wars are an American phenomenon that is being exported to Britain and other countries through **Networked Global Society** (p30) and **Global Culture**. If we follow the American path, these groups in society will become more hostile and extreme.

You can link these findings to **Goodhart**'s idea of the 'Somewheres' vs the 'Anywheres' (p16) and also to **Laclau & Mouffe**'s idea that **Post-Marxism** needs to focus on new 'antagonisms' (p43) to mobilise the Moderates and the Disengaged.

Research: political correctness, the Culture Wars in the USA, more about Social Justice and 'Woke,' recent culture wars over statue toppling, pronouns, the Royal Family, Hollywood movies and TV shows (e.g. *Friends*)

IMPACT ON CULTURE: CULTURAL HOMOGENISATION

An alternative view is that the rise of the Internet accelerates a trend towards homogenisation – which means the tendency for things to become more similar. This means that increasingly people are becoming more similar in their views, tastes, lifestyle and behaviour: they wear the same brands, eat the same food, watch the same shows and have the same outlook. The homogenous culture that everyone is adopting is usually described as a Western, Capitalist culture – or more specifically an American culture.

The opposite is **cultural heterogenisation** – which means the tendency for society to become more **multicultural** and diverse.

This links to **Giddens (1990**, p10**)** who claims that a Cosmopolitan outlook is emerging that is tolerant and individualistic – although **Giddens (2017)** warns that we might face a *"Cosmopolitan overload"* and a return to traditional thinking (nationalism, religious fundamentalism).

This leads to two questions: (1) **is cultural homogenisation actually happening?** (2) **is that a good thing or a bad thing?**

Homogenous culture might be a good thing if it brought people together, gave them less to fight over, reduced misunderstandings and suspicion and enabled people to travel and mix more easily. However, it would be a bad thing if it led to local cultures being extinguished, religions and languages dying out and the replacement of interesting and meaningful traditions with a bland and shallow **Consumer Culture** that leaves everyone unfulfilled.

Conflict sociologists are particularly concerns that the ***problems*** of Western culture will be exported to the rest of the world, spreading inequality, racism, sexism and exploitation. Other sociologists argue that Western culture can export the ***solutions*** to these problems: human rights, Black Lives Matter, Feminism and democracy.

McDonald's in Osaka, Japan

AO2 ILLUSTRATION: McDONALD'S

McDonald's is a fast food restaurant chain founded by two brothers, Dick and Mac McDonald, in 1940. There are now 36,000 restaurants in 100 countries serving 69 million customers. It delivers a standardised menu (e.g. the Big Mac burger) within a standardised architectural space (the iconic 'Golden Arches' and mansard-style roof, brick walls, Colonial windows).

McDonald's has become a symbol of **Globalisation** and, in 1986, UK campaigners distributed leaflets entitled **'What's wrong with McDonald's — everything they don't want you to know,'** accusing the company of ruining the environment and exploiting workers in developing countries. McDonald's sued them and the trial lasted years. The British court ruled that McDonald's wasn't to blame for deforestation or starvation but had deliberately depressed wages in the food industry.

Super Size Me (2004, dir. Morgan Spurlock) is a documentary film in which Spurlock lived on nothing but McDonald's food for a month; he gained 18 pounds and became depressed. McDonald's later removed the 'supersize' option from the menu, triggering a shift towards clean eating and healthier fast food. This shows Globalisation promoting an unhealthy fast food culture – but also Global Media challenging that culture, leading to reform.

RESEARCH PROFILE: FRIEDMAN (1999)

Thomas Friedman wrote about Globalisation in **The Lexus & the Olive Tree (1999)**; the Lexus motor car symbolises the drive for prosperity and the olive tree symbolises the love of tradition. In one chapter, Friedman argues for the benefits of Globalisation, stating that no country with a McDonald's in it has gone to war with another country with a McDonalds in it. This is jokingly referred to as **'the Golden Arches Theory of Conflict Prevention.'**

Friedman's theory is that a country has to reach a certain level of economic development with a large middle class before McDonald's will set up a network of restaurants there. Countries that reach this level become **'McDonald's countries'** and are no longer motivated to fight wars with their neighbours because they can trade instead.

This is part of a wider argument that Globalisation creates economic ties between countries that make it not worthwhile fighting wars.

There are counter examples to Friedman's theory, not least that, soon after his book was published, NATO bombed Yugoslavia and a mob in Belgrade demolished the McDonald's restaurants there. Similarly in 1999, India and Pakistan fought a war over Kashmir and more recently in 2022 Russia invaded Ukraine.

Friedman admits his theory was *"slightly tongue-in-cheek"* but has updated it with the Dell Theory, pointing out that countries don't go to war if they are both part of the Dell Computers supply chain – because this shows a level of economy connection that makes war irrational.

IMPACT ON CULTURE: CULTURAL DEFENCE (GLOCALISATION)

Cultural Defence is a response to Globalisation. It involves 'doubling down' on features that make your own culture distinctive and intensifying them, while rejecting elements of **Global Culture** that are seen as a threat. **Giddens (1990)** points out that religious **fundamentalism** is a type of Cultural Defence (p10): people who are disturbed by **de-traditionalisation** place a much stronger emphasis on their religious traditions than previously and view the encroaching Global Culture as 'unholy' or 'blasphemous.'

Other types of Cultural Defence include insistence on speaking (and making sure your children speak) your native language, wearing traditional clothes, preserving traditional gender roles (such as making sure wives and daughters stay at home) and preserving traditional crafts. You will notice that Cultural Defence can be good or bad. **National Identity** can be part of Cultural Defence, with people becoming more nationalistic in the face of foreign influences.

One way of overcoming Cultural Defence is a strategy known as **glocalisation**, combining Globalisation with local culture. Companies do this to make their products seem less 'foreign' and threatening, for example Domino's succeeded in India by using regional recipes in its pizzas, such as green bananas with chiles, and Nike's 'Year of the Rat' sneakers were popular in China.

A positive view of glocalisation is that it is a sensitive balance of Global Culture while observing local traditions. A more negative view is that it manipulates consumers by offering something superficially familiar in order to make profits for big Capitalist companies.

*This is similar to the debate about Hybrid Culture vs Cultural Appropriation you encountered in **1A: Socialisation, Culture & Identity**.*

Chicken Maharaja Burger (source: McDonald's)

AO2 ILLUSTRATION: McDONALD'S continued

Although McDonald's has a standardised architecture and menu worldwide, it does vary its menu to allow for local traditions. In Japan, there is a **Teriyaki Mac Burger** which is a "*juicy pork burger with a garlicky Teriyaki glaze, lemon sauce and lettuce.*" In India, where beef is unpopular with some Hindus and pork is unclean for Muslims, there is a **Chicken Maharaja Mac**. There are **Coconut Pies** in Singapore, Taro Pies in China (taro is a sweet vegetable that is bright purple), a **McFalafel** in Israel, the **McLobster** in Canada, the **McBeer** in Germany (where McDonald's sells alcohol) and the **Bacon Roll** here in the UK.

This **glocalisation** goes back to the early years of McDonald's and explains the **Filet-O-Fish**. This was the first non-hamburger added to the menu in 1963 and was created by a McDonald's restaurant owner named Lou Groen who struggled to sell meat meals to his Catholic customers on Fridays. Adding a 'fish burger' to the menu brought these customers in and it has remained on the menu since. Despite being horrible.

RESEARCH PROFILE: RITZER (1993)

George Ritzer coined the term '**McDonaldisation**' in his book *The McDonaldization of Society* **(1993)**. He builds on **Max Weber**'s idea that society is becoming more rationalist and scientific.

Being American, he also spells McDonaldization the US way – with a z.

Ritzer argues that the organisation of a McDonald's restaurant reflects the organisation of modern society: (1) **Efficiency:** tasks are done as quickly as possible with minimum waste – the fast food experience where your meal comes pre-packaged; (2) **Calculability:** there is a focus on what can be counted (cost, calories, fat content) rather than incalculable things like quality, taste, enjoyment; (3) **Predictability:** a standardised procedure in the kitchen means that every burger comes out identical; (4) **Control:** CCTVs and other devices monitor the staff or employ technology (like touch screen menus) to do away with human staff altogether.

This leads to unskilled workforces who are underpaid for their work, which is boring and repetitive: this work has been termed a '**McJob.**'

McDonaldisation creeps into other aspects of life (like ordering your taxi using an app, online shopping, drive-thru restaurants, self-service tills in supermarkets, microwavable meals, food full of additives and preservatives, online tuition, speed cameras, etc.).

There is also a reaction *against* this soulless system. **De-McDonaldisation** is a type of Cultural Defence that focuses on products that are authentic, traditional crafts, handmade designs and 'artisanal' products with the human touch. For example, many communities protest at the opening of a Starbucks, believing it will close down local tea shops and cafes.

Research: McJobs, protests against Starbucks, complaints about McDonalds; watch *Super Size Me*

IMPACT ON IDENTITY

Identity is introduced in **1A: Socialisation, Culture & Identity** as a person's self-image, brought about through **socialisation**. The **Interactionist Perspective** also suggests that Identity is shaped by ongoing social interactions. **Becker (1963)** proposes **Labelling Theory** to explain how society labels us based on our behaviour and we either negotiate or internalise these labels, leading to the **Self-Fulfilling Prophecy** where we become the thing we were labelled as.

You were also introduced to **Intersectionality**, which proposes that some Identities are privileged but others are **oppressed** or **marginalised**. **Crenshaw (1991)** shows how marginalised Identities intersect for Black women, creating distinctive patterns of oppression which non-women and non-Blacks fail to appreciate.

3rd **Wave Feminism** and **Neo-Marxism** both incorporate these ideas. **McIntosh (1989)** introduced the phrase '**White Privilege'** and Conflict sociologists propose there are many **hegemonic Identities** (White, male, straight, cis, middle class, able-bodied) which enjoy privileges in society that the privileged people do not recognise.

Foucault (1966, p41) adds to this the idea of discourses in society which confer power upon some people and he calls for these discourses to be **deconstructed** (exposed) and **problematised** (dismantled). **Butler (1990)** echoes this idea, calling for the *queer*-ing of masculine and heteronormative values in society (p45).

Digital Forms of Communication (DFOC) have an impact on Identity, either by encouraging Identity to become more fluid or by reinforcing socially normative Identities.

IMPACT ON IDENTITY: SOCIAL CLASS

Class Identity is introduced in **1A: Socialisation, Culture & Identity**, with the three-tier class system of working classes doing manual work, educated middle classes doing office work and the ruling classes inheriting their wealth. **Savage et al. (2013)** conducted the **Great British Class Survey** and added more classes, like the New Affluent Workers and the struggling Precariat.

Social class is judged by others based on factors like the way you dress and especially the way you talk. In the UK, accent is a very strong indicator of class and working class people used to take elocution lessons to adopt a more middle class manner that would give them opportunities.

DFOC removes these class indicators, because communicating through text doesn't reveal accent and the casual conventions of text-speak (and use of emojis) removes indicators of educational level too. Online identities can have a new name and an avatar instead of a personal photograph – and even digital images are easily manipulated to make a person seem more glamorous. This ought to have a **levelling effect** (making everyone on the same level).

AO2 ILLUSTRATION: ONLINE ACTIVISM & SOCIAL JUSTICE

Online activism is working to bring about political change using DFOC. 'Activism' can mean a range of things, from opposing racism to supporting it. **Social Justice** is a particular type of political activism that opposes discrimination and seeks a fairer society.

Social Justice involves (1) fighting for **human rights**; (2) demanding **access** (food, housing, healthcare, education) for marginalised groups; (3) encouraging **participation** – making sure the voices of marginalised groups are heard; (4) demanding **equity** [see below].

Equity is the most controversial aspect of Social Justice. It is not the same as 'equality.' Equality involves making sure everyone gets the same things but equity is making sure people get what they need – that involves giving special help to the most marginalised people but not giving that same help to people who are already privileged. It is sometimes called **'positive discrimination'** (or **'affirmative action'** in the USA) since it involves discriminating in favour of marginalised groups. For example, making sure universities offer more places to students from working class or ethnic minority backgrounds.

*You should be able to see that Social Justice is linked to **Intersectionality** (p24) and forms part of the **Culture Wars** (p46). In **Section B**, it relates to Left Wing views on crime and deviance (p135).*

RESEARCH PROFILE: TUFECKI (2017)

Zeynap Tufecki is a Turkish sociologist who wrote **Twitter & Tear Gas** (**2017**) in which she analyses the link between online activism and public protest. She draws on her own experience of the **2011 'Arab Spring'** when protestors in Africa and the Middle East rose up against their regimes, demanding more freedom and justice for the poor. She also explores the **2011 Occupy Wall Street (OWS)** movement in New York which campaigned against Capitalism, the **2013 Gezi Park protests** for greater freedom in Turkey and the **Black Lives Matter** movement.

Tufecki points out these online movements are **decentralised** (leaderless, not organised) and this enables them to spring into action very quickly but suffer **'tactical freezes'** – they cannot change strategy or negotiate demands: *"Older movements had to build their organizing capacity first, modern networked movements can scale up quickly … without building any substantial organizational capacity before the first protest or march."*

A different explanation of the failure of online activism to achieve political goals is offered by **Evgeny Morozov (2011)** who blames **'slactivism'** – online activism involves clicking likes or texting support, which makes the activist feel good but involves no real commitment.

Research: Arab Spring, Occupy Wall Street (and other Occupy movements, e.g. in London), Gezi Park, Black Lives Matter (e.g. Ferguson protests, George Floyd's murder), Extinction Rebellion, the 2018-19 Yellow Vest protests in France, the 2019-20 Hong Kong protests

IMPACT ON IDENTITY: GENDER

Gender Identity is introduced in **1A: Socialisation, Culture & Identity**, with the idea that **sex** is **binary** (male and female) and biological but **gender** (what is considered masculine and feminine behaviour) is a **social construct**. Traditional (materialist) **Feminism** sees gender as an oppressive construct, forcing women into subordinate roles and justifying male privilege and power.

Many **3rd** and **4th Wave Feminists** reject this analysis. Instead, they view gender as a **spectrum**, allowing for many gender identities. Extreme forms of this **Gender Identity Theory** view sex as a spectrum too. Materialist Feminists (who term themselves as **Gender Critical**) criticise this for removing what defines a woman – her biology. Supporters argue that Gender Identity Theory is important for achieving **Social Justice** (p53) for non-binary women and Trans women and they criticise Gender Critical Feminists as being **TERF**s (**Trans-Excluding Radical Feminists**).

Gender Identity Theory is particularly popular in **online activism**, because DFOC makes it easy for a person to identify differently from how they are perceived to be in their offline life.

AO2 ILLUSTRATION: MUMSNET CONTROVERSIES

Mumsnet is a **Virtual Community** (p35) and a vertical **Social Media** platform (p34), bringing together women and parents for discussion, support and activism. It was founded in 2000 by **Justine Roberts** and has become very influential – before UK elections, political leaders are often interviewed on *Mumsnet* and it has led campaigns for children with disabilities and care after miscarriages. It has 4.3 million users a month, posting over 35,000 messages a day.

Mumsnet is sometimes criticised for contributing to stereotypical ideas about femininity and motherhood. For example, in 2013 the celebrity Amanda Holden was condemned by Mumsnetters for returning to work (on *Britain's Got Talent*) too soon after having a baby.

On the other hand, *Mumsnet* is also a focus for Feminist online activism, but this has led to controversy. *Mumsnet* is criticised for allowing **transphobic** discussion. Journalist **Eve Livingstone** (2018) accuses *Mumsnet* as being *"a toxic hotbed of transphobia"* and companies like *Flora* margarine have boycotted promotions organised by *Mumsnet* because of such allegations. Justine Roberts insists *Mumsnet* is only allowing free speech and debate over Gender Identity, including respecting the views of Gender Critical Feminists.

RESEARCH PROFILE: HARAWAY (1985)

Donna Haraway wrote *A Cyborg Manifesto* (1985) arguing for the positive role that science and technology can have for female Identity. Haraway's *Manifesto* pre-dates the invention of the World Wide Web but it is way ahead of its time.

Haraway argues against **essentialism** – the idea that there is anything that absolutely defines what it is to be a woman. This is an insight that was taken up by **3**[rd] and **4**[th] **Wave Feminists** and Gender Identity Theory. She regards language itself as 'coded' with patriarchal meanings which women need to break free from; this is similar to **Foucault**'s discourses (p41) and the Queer Theory of **Judith Butler** (p45).

She uses the Science Fiction idea of a **cyborg** – a creature part human, part machine – to describe how a woman could leave gender behind and why Feminism should bring together different Identities under its cause. This insight was taken up by **Intersectionality** and is similar to **Laclau & Mouffe**'s recommendations for **Post-Marxism** (p43).

Haraway's cyborg seems to be an imaginative metaphor for combining and changing Identities – she's not *literally* claiming women should turn themselves into machines! However, the **Digital Revolution** (p28) has given a new meaning to her ideas. **Amber Case (2007)** argues that DFOC enables people to express themselves through machines (computers) and that **Virtual Communities** (p35) are rather like Haraway's cyborgs, where technology helps people leave their gendered bodies behind and define their own Identities.

Research: the debate over Gender Critical Feminists/TERFS – but be warned, you will come across strong language on both sides

IMPACT ON IDENTITY: AGE

Age Identity is introduced in **1A: Socialisation, Culture & Identity**, with the idea of maturation being a biological change but Age as a social construct, putting people into categories like Child, Youth, Adult, Middle Aged and Elderly. **Postman (1994)** argues that Childhood is disappearing because of new technologies like TV and computers and the new relationships created by DFOC.

Research: review your notes on **Postman**'s *Disappearance of Childhood* from **1A** and apply them to DFOC. If you studied **Youth Subcultures** in **1B**, review your notes on **Maffesoli**'s **Neo-Tribes** and apply that to DFOC too.

Postmodernists think that DFOC have accelerated the **fragmentation** of age groupings that used to be 'written in stone.' Instead, age is a **fluid** Identity: adults (sometimes termed '**kidults**') play online video games or follow movie franchises enjoyed by children (e.g. *Star Wars* or *Harry Potter*), middle aged people listen to pop music and join fan subcultures (e.g. K-Pop or Japanese anime) and elderly people use online dating to enjoy romance and sex.

Critical Perspectives have a similar view about DFOC changing Age Identities. **Marxists** argue that elderly people are discarded by society when they stop contributing to Capitalism by working; **Feminists** argue middle aged women are discarded when the menopause makes them no longer fertile (and therefore no longer desired by men). DFOC allow older people to continue to be socially, economically and politically active.

On the other hand, the Elderly can be a **Digital Underclass** (p61) who are cut off from DFOC because they lack the skills to make use of the Internet.

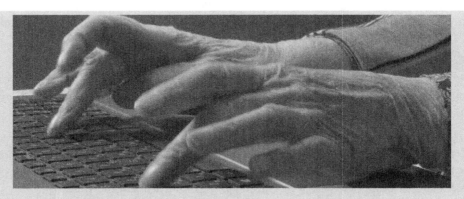

AO2 ILLUSTRATION: GREY POWER & NOSTALGIA

The **Grey Pound** is an expression for the economic power of the Elderly. In the past, the Elderly were referred to as 'pensioners' and seen as poor, but since the **2008 Global Financial Crisis (GFC)** the Elderly have become better-off compared to the young. *Saga*, a company offering leisure products for the Elderly, estimates in 2020 that the Grey Pound is worth £320 billion a year. This increased during the 2020-22 Coronavirus Pandemic as older people embraced DFOC and Internet shopping.

Linked to this is the idea of **Grey Power**: as people live longer but have fewer children, the Elderly become a larger proportion of the population. Moreover, they are the group most likely to vote in elections. This means politicians are under pressure to pass laws that keep the Elderly happy. The politicians themselves tend to be old: Donald Trump was the oldest President to be inaugurated at 70 until Joe Biden replaced him, aged 78.

A motivating factor for many older people is **nostalgia** – a sentimental and affectionate view of the past. The political influence of nostalgia could explain the 2016 election of Donald Trump ('Make American Great Again') and the Brexit Referendum result, a result that politician **Vince Cable (2018)** blamed on *"nostalgia for a world where passports were blue, faces were white and the map was coloured imperial pink."*

Capitalism exploits nostalgia in its advertising: TV ads featuring *Top Cat* and the *Flintstones*, *Adidas* re-releasing *Superstars* and *Gazelle* trainers or the success of *Pokémon Go* in 2016. If society is dominated by **uncertainty** (p41) and **risk** (p10), then nostalgia is an important source of security for a growing number of people.

RESEARCH PROFILE: PAGE (2019)

Ben Page is the head of the survey company Ipsos Mori who collaborated with the Centre for Ageing Better to produce *The Perennials: the future of ageing* (**2019**). 'Perennial' is a term coined to mean the opposite of the youthful Millennials born in the 1980s and '90s.

Page cites an Ipso Mori **Global Trends Survey** which found 49% of UK respondents would like their country to be 'the way it used to be' but this rose to 58% for the over-60s.

The survey also found that on average 'Old Age' starts at 74 in Spain but 55 in Saudi Arabia, 61 for the under 24s but 72 for the over-55s. This shows the **social construction** of Age Identity. The report agrees that older people are 'airbrushed' out of the Media: only 1.5% of TV characters are Elderly and most have minor roles.

The report concludes that despite negative stereotypes of ageing, old age is becoming a time of opportunity for many people.

Research: more examples of nostalgia in advertising; the *Friends* reunion; bands doing comeback tours; nostalgia music and TV channels

IMPACT ON INEQUALITY

Inequality is introduced in **2B: Understanding Social Inequalities** as a person's life chances that can be improved by work, wealth and education or held back by discrimination or lack of opportunity. **Meritocracy** is an understanding that society is structured to reward talent and hard work, but **Bourdieu (1984)** argues that society is structured around **Social Reproduction**, ensuring that inequalities are reproduced from one generation to the next.

Marxists identify the root cause of this inequality in **Capitalism**. Many **Feminists** would agree but insist that women are subject to even greater inequality, since they are subordinate to men in a **Patriarchal** society.

Intersectionality proposes that some Identities are privileged but others are **oppressed** or **marginalised**. Critical theories explain inequalities through this intersection of oppression for some people and **unearned privilege** for others.

Applied Postmodernism (e.g. **Post-Marxism** and **3rd** or **4th Wave Feminism**) identifies the source of oppression in language itself. It calls for **deconstructing**, **problematising** or *queer*-ing the taken-for-granted assumptions in language to draw attention to inequality and demolish the justifications for it.

Digital Forms of Communication (DFOC) have an impact on Identity, either by encouraging Identity to become more fluid or by reinforcing socially normative Identities.

IMPACT ON INEQUALITY: SOCIAL CLASS

DFOC allows people to educate themselves, find work, find good deals on purchases or get help with problems. People without wealth or **Social Capital** (p21) can promote themselves online, gather followers and acquire influence. This should be **empowering** the working classes.

On the other hand, access to **Digital Social Networks** requires money (for computers, tablets or smartphones as well as broadband access) and skills. This leads to a **Digital Divide** between people with the technology and skills to benefit from DFOC and those without. Moreover, Capitalist businesses use DFOC to exploit working class people. Online gambling was worth £5.7 billion in the UK in 2020 and people from deprived backgrounds spend more on 'virtual slot machines' that are particularly addictive (source: the **Gambling Commission**).

AO2 ILLUSTRATION: UBER & THE GIG ECONOMY

Uber is a US Tech company founded in 2009 whose mobile app puts customers in touch with taxi drivers or food delivery firms. Uber takes a 25% cut for the service. It is the largest company operating in the '**gig economy.**' The gig economy is an arrangement where people work flexible hours providing on-demand services, with DFOC putting them in touch with customers or employers. Tech companies make a profit from each transaction. For employers, the gig economy lets them hire workers for single tasks (like a digital artist or delivery driver) without taking them on as a full-time employee. For customers, it means a worker (like a taxi driver) can be hired quickly at low cost.

The gig economy means workers can get work quickly and only work the hours they choose to work. However, gig workers don't get the holidays, pensions, sickness benefits and other legal protections that full-time workers do, even if they work full-time hours.

Critics claim that the gig economy exploits the poorest workers, giving them no rights and forcing them to work long hours to support themselves. Uber claims it is just a booking agent and the taxi drivers are all self-employed protection. However, in 2021 the **UK Supreme Court** ruled that Uber is in fact an employer and must protect its drivers. Cities like London have tried to ban Uber, to protect the rights of taxi drivers and protect passengers.

Uber in Beijing (photo: bfishadow)

RESEARCH PROFILE: BURGESS (2020)

Gemma Burgess reports on an ongoing research project into the digital divide carried out by **Cambridge University**. She argues that the divide has been worsened by the 2020-22 Coronavirus Pandemic.

Burgess points out the using DFOC requires a range of **digital skills** (communication by text, using search engines, buying or downloading from the World Wide Web, problem solving, staying safe online) as well as access to expensive technology. She concludes that **digital exclusion** affects a fifth of the UK population, with 8% of people having zero digital skills and 12% being limited in digital skills. Of the 8 million people in the UK without access to the Internet, 90% are economically deprived.

The Covid Pandemic increased the importance of **Digital Social Networks** (working or studying online and staying in contact with friends and family through DFOC), so this has increased the exclusion for 20% of people with limited or no digital skills.

Research: controversies about Uber; the gig economy; problems with online gambling

IMPACT ON INEQUALITY: GENDER

DFOC allows women to study, find work, find good deals on purchases or get help with problems like domestic violence. **Social Media** (p34) provides support for women – such as **Mumsnet** (p54). Online activism raises the awareness of problems facing women, such as the **Everyday Sexism Project** (p25). This should be **empowering** for women.

On the other hand, the Internet can be a hostile place for women. Internet Trolls frequently target women with rape threats. Revenge Porn is used by embittered former partners who upload sexually explicit images relating to women they are angry about. The Internet makes it easier for stalkers to harass women and sex-traffickers to exploit women.

The World Wide Web hosts a lot of pornography and the most visited pornography website, *Pornhub*, gets as much traffic as *Netflix* or *Linkedin*. It is estimated that 1 in 7 web searches is for pornography. A report from **Ofsted (2021)** claims school-age boys collect pornography on their mobile phones and use it for sexual bullying of girls: 9 in 10 school-age girls report sexist bullying and being sent unwanted pornographic images.

Feminists are divided over the issue of pornography. Traditional (materialist) Feminists tend to be anti-porn, viewing it as the exploitation and objectification of women's bodies and linking it to violent and **misogynistic** (women-hating) attitudes in society. However, some 4th Wave Feminists are in favour of 'sex-positive' pornography that empowers women or *queer*-ing **heteronormative** sexuality (heterosexual, male-centred) through porn.

AO2 ILLUSTRATION: TROLLS, THE MANOSPHERE & INCELS

An Internet **'Troll'** is someone who posts messages on **Social Media** (p34) or **Virtual Communities** (p35) to provoke or upset other people, usually to get attention for themselves but sometimes to damage someone's reputation or interfere with politics. The worst Trolling involves very offensive threats, including death threats, and **slurs** (offensive names, often sexist, racist, homophobic or transphobic). Trolling is a type of **cyber-bullying**. Trolling is particularly common on anonymous online forums (like *Reddit* or *4chan*), *Twitter* and anonymous *YouTube* comments.

Misogynist (women-hating) trolling is a growing problem. In 2020, the Australian *Herald Sun* had to close its comments section on women's football coverage because of offensive trolling. According to a **2020 BBC Survey**, 30% of British sportswomen report being trolled on social media, with offensive remarks about their appearance and attractiveness, up from 14% in 2015. Trolls also target women with rape threats.

Some of this trolling comes from anti-Feminist virtual communities known as the **'manosphere.'** These groups tend to be traditionalists in the **Culture Wars** (p46) and some are **Alt-Right** extremists. **Incels** are an exceptionally misogynistic virtual community regarded by many as a hate group or even as terrorists. Incel stands for 'involuntary celibate' as they blame women for not providing them with sex. Incels go beyond trolling: since 2014 there have been at least 7 mass murders and 56 deaths caused by men who were involved with the Incel movement online.

> **Research:** refer to your notes on **Faludi (1999)** in **1A: Socialisation, Culture & Identity**; is the 'backlash' against Feminism and the misogyny she detected in American men present online?

RESEARCH PROFILE: MOLONEY & LOVE (2018)

Mairead Moloney & Tony Love studied the increase in misogynist trolling in social media. They identify (1) **online sexual harassment**, pestering women for sexual relations (such as sending nude images); (2) **gendertrolling**, which is targeting non-conforming or successful women for trolling; (3) **e-bile**, which is personal abuse and sexual slurs; (4) **disciplinary rhetoric**, meaning death or rape threats to silence women.

Moloney & Love take an **Interactionist** approach, looking at **'Virtual Manhood Acts'** (VMA). Manhood Acts are behaviours which **enforce hegemonic gender norms** (i.e. they oppress women and elevate men as well as oppressing anyone falling outside traditional binary ideas of gender). VMA can be textual (writing), verbal (spoken) or visual (images).

They conclude that the same interactions take place online as in the offline world and their purpose is to keep men "in the box." This is the idea that traditional masculinity occupies a 'box' a deviating outside of the box makes a person **effeminate** or **queer**. Men police the borders of the 'box' and use slurs and labels for those outside it (women, LGBT people, disabled people, etc.). Online fluid identities make it harder to keep men "in the box" which explains the hostility and aggression on VMA towards women.

IMPACT ON INEQUALITY: AGE

DFOC allows older people to shop, seek relationships or get help with problems. DFOC allows people who are no longer economically active to promote themselves online, gather followers and acquire influence. This should be **empowering** the Elderly.

On the other hand, access to **Digital Social Networks** requires skills the Elderly often lack. They have been termed a **Digital Underclass** – as opposed to the young who grew up after the **Digital Revolution** (p28) who are **Digital Natives**. For example, 99% of adults (aged 16-34) use the Internet at least once every three months, but this was only 54% for those aged 75+ (source: **ONS, 2019**). However, this was an increase from only 20% of 75+ people in 2011.

Don't confuse the Digital Underclass with the New Right's idea of the Underclass. The Digital Underclass are people who don't go online – it's nothing to do with single parents on benefits!

AO2 ILLUSTRATION: THE ELDERLY DURING LOCKDOWN

During the **2020-22 Coronavirus Pandemic**, the UK and other countries imposed Lockdowns: people were asked to stay at home and avoid contact with friends, neighbours and family members. This had a big impact on the Elderly who already suffer social isolation (due to family growing up and moving away, peers or partners becoming ill or dying, retirement, etc).

Many people turned to DFOC to stay in touch with family and support groups. Daily users of the video app *Zoom* went from 10 million to 200 million during 2020.

Many older people turned to online shopping to get their groceries without the risk of going to supermarkets. Online shopping by the over-75s increased by 24% after the Lockdowns started (source: **Age UK**). However, Age UK claims this increase in Internet usage has mostly come from existing Internet users going online more often. The shift to online shopping is in fact leaving many older people behind. Age UK trains volunteers to become 'Digital Buddies' for the elderly in their community and help them get online.

RESEARCH PROFILE: HU & QIAN (2021)

Canadian researchers **Yang Hu & Yue Qian** argue that over-60s dependent on online contact felt more lonely during Lockdown. They survey 5148 people aged 60+ in the UK and 1391 in the US, both before and during Lockdown. The increase in loneliness was *higher* for those who reported more virtual contact. This supports a **cultural pessimist** view of DFOC (p39).

The findings only show that virtual contact is *associated* with loneliness - not that it is the cause. People who feel more isolated to start with will make virtual contact more frequently. But it shows that virtual contact on its own is not beneficial to older people's mental health –there is an improvement when online contact is supplemented by face-to-face contact.

IMPACT ON RELATIONSHIPS

The impact of DFOC on relationships illustrates the difference between **neophiles** and **cultural pessimists** (p39).

Neophiles see DFOC as beneficial for our relationships. Through **Digital Social Networks** we can have more relationships, maintain relationships at a distance and have new types of relationships. Examples include video conferencing at work or in education, online dating and the membership of **virtual communities** (e.g. a 'guild' in *World of Warcraft*, p35). They see these online relationships as just as valuable, productive and satisfying as face-to-face relationships.

Cultural Pessimists see DFOC as unsatisfactory substitutes for 'real' or face-to-face relationships: they are inauthentic, shallow and full of deception and confusion. Pessimists point out that online friends are not really emotionally committed to you and may not be who they claim to be. Your privacy can be hacked and your identity stolen. The **Twitter-storms** (p34) and **Trolling** (p60) that goes on online can be immensely stressful and hurtful. Because of the anonymity online, people can be unrestrained and extreme in their behaviour. **Sherry Turkle (2011)** warns that online relationships make us *"alone together"* (the title of her book, which links to Putnam's *Bowling Alone*, p22) – despite receiving daily emails and chatting online, people become isolated and lonely.

Postmodernists are positive about online relationships, but **Zygmunt Bauman (2013)** is aware of the uncertainty involved in them – but he argues this uncertainty is now a characteristic of *all* our relationships. For example, in the UK 42% of marriages end in divorce (source: **ONS, 2019**).

4th Wave Feminists are also positive about online relationships because of the possibility of defining your own identity and sharing experiences of oppression. For example, **Laura Bates' Everyday Sexism Project** allows women to share their testimonies of harassment, discrimination and abuse. However, the rise of **misogynistic Trolls** and **Incels** (p60) shows that toxic relationships get a boost from the Internet too.

Post-Marxists see the benefits of online relationships to organise **Social Justice** activism (p53) and challenge the **hegemonic discourses** (p42) that shape face-to-face relationships. However, because so much of the Internet is controlled by the big Tech companies and so much online content is created by big Media companies, Capitalist values (advertising, shopping, branding, stereotyping) are very influential online too.

AO2 ILLUSTRATION: ONLINE DATING & TINDER

Organised 'matchmaking' has been around since the 19th century, but online dating began with *Kiss.com* (1994), followed by sites like *Match.com* (1995), *Gaydar* (1999), *eHarmony* (2000) and *Grindr* (2009). These sites use mathematical calculations (algorithms) to match people by their preferences and interests.

Tinder was launched in 2012 and is an app that lets you match yourself with other users by swiping on their profile picture: users who match each other are put into contact.

The popularity of these sites is growing: between 2015-19 32% of new couples met online, an increase from 19% between 2005-14 (source: **Statistia**). *Tinder* hit a record 3 billion swipes on one day in March 2020 and has broken that record hundreds of times since then.

Not all online dating experiences are positive. 57% of female online daters experience harassment (source: **Pew, 2020**). Catfishing is when someone adopts a fake identity to manipulate a dating partner – either to exploit them sexually or cheat them out of money. There can be long-term trauma and depression after being victimised like this.

Three Chechen girls 'catfished' the terror group Islamic State (ISIS) by pretending to be recruited on **Social Media**, giving the recruiters fake names and photographs, taking $3300 to travel to the Middle East, then keeping the money and closing their accounts (source: **RT News, 2015**). No one feels sorry for terror groups who get swindled this way, but it illustrates the potential for deception and exploitation in online dating.

RESEARCH PROFILE: MILLER (2011)

Daniel Miller wrote *Tales From Facebook* (**2011**) drawing on interviews with *Facebook* users in Trinidad. *Facebook* is the world's largest **Social Media** site which went public in 2006 and has 2.8 billion daily users worldwide (source: **Statistia, 2020**) – although there were 'only' 500 million users when Miller carried out his research.

One is an ageing man who uses Facebook to get over his constraints; another is a young man who finds comfort and a **Virtual Community** in the online game *Farmville*; there is also a Christian who uses *Facebook* to evangelise and stay in touch with other church members.

Miller argues that *Facebook* restores close social relationships that were previously declining and brings people together over great distances.

However, he also observes how *Facebook* posts revealed an affair, leading to the break-up of a marriage, and observes the consequences for a music star who has had a sex video leaked – both having effects offline as well as online.

Miller focuses entirely on *Facebook* as a **Digital Social Network** rather than a Capitalist business that makes profits from advertising. **Marxists** would draw attention to the controversies about *Facebook*-users losing their privacy and the company treating them as commodities to advertisers – and sharing data about its users with companies like *Amazon* and *Netflix* (source: **New York Times, 2018**).

Neither does Miller analyse the sexism going on in *Facebook* discourses from a **Feminist** perspective – such as the analysis carried out by **Moloney & Love** (p60).

Conclusions about the Impact of Digital Forms of Communication

Many social scientists (sociologists and psychologists) suspect that **digital forms of communication** don't just let us communicate faster, more easily, with more people – they actually change the way we feel about ourselves and relate to each other.

Neophiles hope that these changes are for the best. They claim that the Internet is making us all more politically engaged. It is easy to get involved in online activism, hard to stay ignorant of crimes and corruption going on in society and the Internet provides a powerful way for protesters to catch the attention of politicians and team up with activists in other countries to create a truly worldwide movement.

Even though Globalisation threatens to make everyone **homogenous** (p48), the Internet enables local communities to band together, assert their identities and preserve their traditions through **cultural defence** (p50). This is particularly true for communities who exist as a diaspora – as a scattering of families spread over many countries due to migration.

Women in particular have used this new technology to empower themselves and raise awareness of how they are mistreated. **4th Wave Feminism** has made full use of the Internet to bring women together and share experiences like everyday sexism and #MeToo. It has also joined with activists from other backgrounds in the **Social Justice** movement (p53) which aims to get equity for marginalised people.

However, not everything is so positive. The sort of engagement people make with online causes is often shallow and temporary – slacktivism, not activism. The blending of local cultures with Global Culture is often a cynical marketing ploy by **Trans National Corporations (TNCs)** to sell their products to resisting markets. **Glocalisation** (p50) only happens in ways that suit big businesses.

Moreover, Social Justice isn't the only movement to get empowered online. The Alt-Right is also active on the Internet, with many groups promoting White Supremacy, homophobia and transphobia, as well as religious fundamentalist groups with violent or bigoted agendas. The Internet has no favourites and it empowers the bad as well as the good.

All of this assumes that everyone can actually get online. There is a **Digital Underclass** (p61) of people who cannot afford the modern technology or lack the skills to use it effectively. There are many vulnerably people ready to be exploited online, either by cash-grabbing companies, hoaxes, gambling sites, credit companies or aggressive **Trolls** (p60). Online hate doesn't stay online: it spills onto the streets in mass shootings and bombings. There is also pornography, which is said to make up 35% of all Internet downloads.

It seems the Internet is a mixed blessing because its amazing potential is put to use by people with different agendas: online, as in offline life, the groups with the most money to spend have the biggest influence.

EXAM PRACTICE: IMPACT OF DIGITAL COMMUNICATION

The OCR exam has three questions in **Paper 3 Section A**:

Source A	Source B
Not everyone enjoys the connectedness and fast-paced change of the 21st century. Some see it as a threat to their traditional values and worry that their children will be lured away from their culture by fashion, advertising, video games and travel. One response to this is religious fundamentalism, which rejects the modern world as sinful. However, even fundamentalists use the Internet, to preach their vision of the righteous life, to recruit new members and to condemn the changes that cause them such distress.	There are over 7000 languages in the world, but over half of the population speak just ten – like English, Spanish, Mandarin or Arabic – as their native language. Minority languages are dying out and one 'dies' every week. However, language learning websites and apps are keeping minority languages alive. Online communities promote their language and the culture it expresses, like the Digital Himalayas project, the Diyari blog, the Arctic Languages Vitality project and the Enduring Voices Project.

1. With references to the Source[s], define what sociologists mean by cultural defence. **[9 marks: 5 AO1 + 4 AO2]**

*Make two sociological points about cultural defence, one based on Source A and one on Source B. You should quote from the source. It's not vital to refer to named sociologists but you should definitely use some sociological terminology. Then offer examples of cultural defence and make sure each example has an explanation of **why** it is cultural defence. For example, "Creating an app to teach children your language so your culture won't die out when you pass away."*

2. With references to the Source[s], to what extent do digital forms of communication promote cultural defence? **[10 marks: 4 AO1 + 2 AO2 + 4 AO3]**

Write a paragraph about source A then another about source B. Sum up what's in the source and explain what named sociologists would say about it. Then finish off with a brief evaluation of each view (p66). Make sure you conclude by answering the question (it does promote cultural defence, or it doesn't or perhaps it only partially promotes defence but also undermines it).

3. Evaluate the view that digital forms of communication have a positive impact on people's identities. **[16 marks: 4 AO1 + 4 AO2 + 8 AO3]**

*Write three paragraphs. Each paragraph should introduce a sociological idea with some illustration from the real world. Each paragraph should finish off with developed evaluation (see **Chapter 4** for this). For example, you could write about social class, gender and age as Identities and the impact on each. Don't forget to answer the question: does the Internet have a positive impact or not?*

CHAPTER 4 – EVALUATION

In **Paper 3 Section A (Globalisation & the Digital Social World)**, question 2 assesses **AO3**/evaluation with the phrase *"to what extent?"* while question 3 asks for a developed evaluation (with the command *"evaluate,"* *"assess"* or *"discuss"*).

'To what extent does not have to be developed or address theoretical issues. It can be a common-sense comment. It should be a simple **strength**, **weakness** or **comparison**.

A developed evaluation needs to address theoretical or methodological issues. It needs to go deeper than a 'brief evaluation' and look at an issue from alternative perspectives or work through the implications of a viewpoint.

Here are some evaluative positions candidates can adopt:

Brief Evaluations

These points are suitable for Q2. You can use them in Q3 as well, but their simplicity makes them hard to turn into developed points, so you might miss out on the higher AO3 band marks. Still, better to write something than nothing at all.

"Not all people..." / Over-generalising

Structuralist Perspectives (traditional **Marxism** and **Feminism**) are particularly prone to sweeping generalisations. They often claim that everyone is motivated by the same thing or experiences the same oppression or wants the same outcomes. For example, Marxists claim everyone is part of a social class and Feminists claim all women are in some way oppressed.

To evaluate these ideas, point out that not all people fit into this mould. Not all old people use the Internet (p61), not all women experience abuse online (p60) and not all people benefit from Globalisation (p50**Error! Bookmark not defined.**).

If you are writing about some empirical research, point out that its sample group doesn't resemble everyone. Not all *Facebook*-users are from Trinidad like the ones that Daniel Miller studied (p63).

It's important not to be formulaic. Say *why* not all people are like this: give an example of one of the exceptions. Not all people benefit from Globalisation, *because some people find their traditional values threatened by change*. Not all old people use the Internet *because some don't have the computer skills to get online or use apps*.

"It's out-of-date…" / Time-locked

There's a crucial date in the study of digital forms of communication and it is 2005 – the arrival of **Web2.0** (p28). Can studies from before this – or from before the public availability of Web1.0 in 1991, really tell us anything about digital communication today?

To evaluate these studies, point out that so much has changed. In Web2.0 there is much greater interactivity: users can post up comments on sites, use emojis, upload their own media content, manipulate memes or have instant real-time chat and video communication.

Once again, it's important not to be formulaic. Say *why* one of these changes matters for this particular study: give an example of one of the exceptions. Haraway's idea of Cyborgs (p55**Error! Bookmark not defined.**) is out-of-date because *people meet online where their bodies can't be seen and don't define them*. Putnam's *Bowling Alone* (p22) is out-of-date *because there is online activism now so you don't have to leave your home to get involved in civic activities*.

Online doesn't always reflect offline

Sociologists find lots of links between online and offline behaviour, but there are differences too. The way people behave online and the things they watch and do might not have any effect on their offline behaviour.

To evaluate these ideas, point out that people have a completely different social setting offline and can use body language and facial expressions to communicate. They will also be judged on things like their class, race or gender or their disabilities.

It would be formulaic just to say "people might behave differently offline" and leave it at that. Say *why* the offline behaviour might be different: give an example of one of the influences. For example, online activism might just be slacktivism *because getting involved in protests offline might be time-consuming or even dangerous*.

Developing Evaluations

These points are suitable for Q2 and Q3. Their complexity makes them suitable for turning into developed points, so you can qualify for higher AO3 band marks on Q3.

"It's too Structuralist" / Postmodernist critique

Structuralist Perspectives make sweeping generalisations because they study society as a whole and focus on important institutions rather than individual people. The **Postmodern** Perspective criticises this, saying that in the 21st century people are much more individualistic and construct their Identities from lots of different sources rather than being identified purely by their class, gender or age group.

To evaluate these ideas, point out that a Postmodernist approach might be better. Rather than studying the working class or women or the elderly, study people who have a certain lifestyle in common (like vegans, evangelical Christians or fans of online vloggers).

As usual, avoid being formulaic. Say *why* the Postmodern approach would be better: give an example of one of the benefits. Take a Postmodern approach to studying the Gender, *because instead of just categorising people as male or female you can categorise them by lots of different Gender Identities.*

Development

If you bring in Postmodernism as the solution to the problem, don't stop there. You could give examples of studies that incorporate Postmodern ideas (like **Butler** incorporating discourses into her Queer Theory, p45) or explain how later research incorporates aspects of Postmodernism (like **4th Wave Feminism** focusing on people with different Gender Identities).

Alternatively, criticise your own improvement: discuss the drawbacks of using the Postmodernist approach (e.g. the ideas are very vague and subjective and hard to back up with evidence, such as Gender Identities that are hard to define clearly).

"This is similar to…" / Comparisons

Sometimes, different sociologists or different Perspectives end up saying similar things, although usually for different reasons Marxists and Feminists both agree there is propaganda and brainwashing (**ideology**) in the news and in schools. Marxists and Postmodernists both agree that Globalisation is stressful and difficult for people.

To evaluate these ideas, point out the similarity between the sociology you are writing about and another Perspective or research study. If you have explained that Marxists think that Globalisation spreads Capitalism around the world, explain that Postmodernists also think we live in a Hyper-Reality made up of media images from global companies.

As usual, don't be formulaic. Say *why* the two approaches are so similar *or* say why they are also different: give an example. Marxists and Postmodernists agree on Globalisation because they both think it changes the way we live and relate to each other, *although Marxists think this is always an alienating and exploiting arrangement* and *Postmodernists focus more on how so much choice creates uncertainty*.

Development

If you think two Perspectives are similar, don't stop there. You could give examples of studies from each perspective, like **Robinson** writing about the transnational bourgeoisie waging war on humanity (p13) compared to **Bauman**'s concept of uncertainty (p41) or explain how later research incorporates both perspectives, like the Post-Marxists using Applied Postmodernism to promote **Social Justice** (p53).

Alternatively, criticise the very similarity you suggested: discuss the how differences between the two approaches are more important than similarities (Marxists recognise the overall social context of Capitalism, whereas Postmodernists see a fluid and fragmented world with no overall meaning).

"A Intersectionalist would say …" / Intersectional critique

Intersectionality makes a powerful criticism of other Perspectives and especially research from before the 1990s or the 21st century.

Intersectionality proposes that people are privileged or oppressed based on their Identities and the oppressed Identities intersect in ways that intensify the oppression. This is a criticism of Perspectives that view people through a single lens (e.g. just looking at age, or gender, or class).

In order to avoid being formulaic, say *why* an Intersectional approach would be better: give an example of the benefits. Take an Intersectional approach to studying the impact of digital communication, *because it will focus on working class women experience the Internet differently from middle class women – or how older women have different experiences from young women.*

Development

If you think Intersectionality is good, don't stop there. You could give examples of studies from the Intersectionality perspective (like **Butler**'s Queer Theory or **Laclau & Mouffe**'s Post-Marxism, p43) or explain how Intersectionality appears in other perspectives (like how Social Justice's concern for equity combines Intersectionality and Marxism).

Alternatively, criticise the Intersectionality idea you suggested: discuss the flaws with Intersectionality (like the way it draws Feminists' attention away from women and Marxists' focus away from the working class).

"A weakness of this Perspective is ..." / Standard theoretical critiques

Marxism

Marxism ignores progress: In the last 200 years, Capitalist societies have abolished slavery, set up human rights, created a welfare state and free education and healthcare for all. Marxists often talk as if this hasn't happened or as if it happened *in spite of* Capitalism. This pessimistic view of the past and the future perhaps exaggerates social injustice. *However* Intersectionality shows us that these benefits have been enjoyed by people with privileged Identities more than marginalised ones and **Social Justice** aims to change that.

Marxism is a conspiracy theory: It's standard for Marxists to argue that the Media (especially the news) are controlled by a sinister group of billionaires who brainwash everyone through **ideology**. This underestimates the independence of many journalists, teachers and bosses as well as the ability of ordinary people to think for themselves and work out what's true. *However* Post-Marxism reinterprets this as discourses that give privileges to hegemonic groups rather than an actual conspiracy.

Marxists assume class is homogenous: *Homogenous* means 'all the same' and traditional Marxists think that all working class people share the same relationship to labour and power. *However*, **Intersectionality** focuses on oppressed Identities intersecting, distinguishing between working class people who are elderly or female.

Marxism offers no solutions: You don't have to be a Marxist to spot the Capitalism has flaws! Marxists argue that Capitalism is intrinsically rotten and destructive and it needs to be replaced rather than reformed. But replaced with what? Marxism can be accused of criticising Capitalism without offering a coherent alternative. *However*, the **Social Justice** movement has projects to improve equity for marginalised and disadvantaged groups.

Feminism

Feminism ignores biology: Feminists insist that gender is **socially constructed,** and it certainly is up to a point. However, Psychology reveals lots of biological differences in brain structure, hormones and genes between the sexes and it's unlikely that *none* of this makes *any* difference to social behaviour. *However*, Gender Identity theory (popular with 3rd & 4th Wave Feminists) suggests that sex is *not* based on biology at all and **Judith Butler** argues Gender is **performative** (something you do, not something you are).

Feminism ignores progress: In the last century women have won the vote, the right to be educated at university and manage their own affairs. In Britain, the Sexual Discrimination Act (1975) has outlawed sexual discrimination. Feminism can be accused of downplaying this progress and exaggerating the scale of injustice. *However*, **misogynist Trolls** and murderous **Incels** show that there is still violent hatred towards women.

Feminists assume gender is homogenous: As with Marxists and social class, traditional Feminists are accused of treating all women as if they experienced the same oppression – which in practice means assuming that the difficulties of White women are typical for all women. *However,* **3rd & 4th Wave Feminism** incorporates **Intersectionality** which distinguishes between different feminine Identities (e.g. young and elderly women).

Feminists ignore the oppression of men: Feminists sometimes seem to assume that Masculinity is homogenous and all men are complicit in the Patriarchy, but men are much more likely than women to die by violence, to be victims of crime and to work in dangerous conditions. *However,* online sexual abuse, harassment and rape threats are disproportionately aimed at women, not men.

Postmodernism

Postmodernism ignores continuing modernity: The Internet has made huge changes to our lives, along with technology like mobile phones and satellite TV. However, life for many people continues as it did in the 1960s, '70s and '80s: they live in nuclear families, work in factories or offices, take part in religious worship and live in different social classes. Only a minority of people – and perhaps, only in a few big cities – enjoys the unusual, ever-changing, online lifestyles that Postmodernism claims are typical. This is **Giddens'** argument for **Late Modernity**.

Postmodernists reject objective truth: By rejecting **meta-narratives**, Postmodernism rejects objective truth. Nothing is absolutely and provably true, it can only ever be subjective truth (true-for-you or true-as-you-see-it). But how can social problems be solved unless we agree they objectively *are* problems? Why should sociological research be taken seriously if it's only a point of view? How can we tell good points of view from wild conspiracy theories and 'fake news'?

Postmodernism only applies to some topics: Postmodernism is great for explaining shifts in style and fashion, personal Identity, consumer choice and lifestyles, especially online lifestyles. It's less good for tackling the harder topics of poverty, discrimination and violence. It **also lacks political solutions** for tackling these things. *However,* there is now **Applied Postmodernism** found in 3rd & 4th Wave Feminism or Post-Marxism which is more politically active (e.g. the **Social Justice** movement).

EXAM PRACTICE: SECTION A

The OCR exam has three questions in **Paper 3 Section A**:

Source A	Source B
The 2020-22 Coronavirus Pandemic forced many of us to move to online networking. We worked from home, using email and videoconferencing. We studied from home, completing assignments on websites. We socialised in virtual communities and reached out to loved ones through cyberspace. Unable to travel or fly, business meeting moved online and virtual travel guides showed off foreign destinations to home-bound tourists. While the world was locked down, the Internet showed us we were really more connected than ever.	The problem with the Internet is that it offers more to the haves than the have-nots. If you're already well-off and educated, you can take full advantage of the Internet to study, learn new skills, make valuable contacts and find good jobs. The poorest people can't afford powerful smart phones or tablets. Even when they get them, they lack the ability to make full use of them – and online gambling and shopping sites are always there to take their money. Online, we're more unequal than ever.

1. With references to the Source[s], define what sociologists mean by a networked global society. **[9 marks: 5 AO1 + 4 AO2]**

*Make two sociological points about global networks, one based on Source A and one on Source B. You should quote from the source. It's not vital to refer to named sociologists but you should definitely use some sociological terminology. Then offer examples of global networks and make sure each example has an explanation of **why** it is a global network. For example, "Using a Social Media site like Goodwall to find out about jobs and internships in other countries."*

2. With references to the Source[s], to what extent does a networked global society improve people's social capital? **[10 marks: 4 AO1 + 2 AO2 + 4 AO3]**

Write a paragraph about source A then another about source B. Sum up what's in the source and explain what named sociologists would say about it. Then finish off with a brief evaluation of each view (p66). Make sure you conclude by answering the question (it does improve social capital or it doesn't or perhaps it only improves it for some people but not others).

3. Evaluate the view that digital forms of communication have contributed to conflict in the world. **[16 marks: 4 AO1 + 4 AO2 + 8 AO3]**

Write three paragraphs. Each paragraph should introduce a sociological idea with some illustration from the real world. Each paragraph should finish off with developed evaluation (see p70 for this). For example, you could write about the Culture Wars, online hate groups and terrorists organising themselves online. Don't forget to answer the question: does the Internet lead to more conflict or not?

KEY RESEARCH

The 24 studies here cover all the topics that arise in this Section of the exam and they will prove just as useful in other sections too. Start learning them. For each study, I include the key terms, a Perspective (if relevant) and the particular topics it is linked to.

Boyle (2007): demand-led vs supply-led New Media; **Interactionist**; media convergence, p33

Burgess (2020): digital divide, digital skills, digital exclusion; impact on inequality, networked global society, p59

Butler (1990): *Gender Trouble*, performative gender, gendered reality, Queer Theory; **Feminist**; impact on identity & inequality, p45

Castells (2000): *The Information Age*, informational Capitalism, the Information Age; **Neo-Marxism**; networked global society, impact on inequality, p32

Cornford & Robins (1999): evolutionary vs revolutionary New Media; **Marxism**; digital revolution, media convergence, impact on inequality, conflict & change, p29

Curran & Seaton (1991): patterns of ownership, oligarchy; **Marxist**; social media, social capital, impact on equality, cultural homogeneity, conflict & change, p40

Duffy (2021): traditionalists, progressives, moderates & disengaged, culture wars; conflict & change, impact on inequality, p47

Foucault (1966): discourses, regimes of truth, deconstruction, problematising; **Postmodernist**; impact on identity & inequality, p41

Friedman (1999): *Lexus & the Olive* Tree, Golden Arches Theory of conflict prevention; **Functionalist**; cultural homogenisation, p49

Giddens (1999): *Runaway World*, Late Modernity, detraditionalization, cosmopolitanism, manufactured risk; **Interactionist**; defining Globalisation, cultural defence, impact on Identities, p8, p10

Goodhart (2017): *The Road to Somewhere*, Somewheres vs Anywheres; **Functionalism**; defining Globalisation, impact on Identity, conflict & change, p16

Haraway (1985): *A Cyborg Manifesto*, cyborgs; **Feminism**; impact on identity & inequality, conflict & change, p55

Hu & Qian (2021): online loneliness; impact on inequality & relationships, p61

Laclau & Mouffe (1985): *Hegemony & Socialist Strategy*, hegemony, antagonism; **Post-Marxist**; impact on inequality, conflict & change, p43

McLuhan (1964): global village, the medium is the message; **Interactionist**; global village, impact on identity & relationships, cultural homogeneity; p30

Miller (2011): *Tales From Facebook*; **Interactionist**; social media, virtual community, impact on relationships, p63

Moloney & Love (2018): Virtual Manhood Acts (VMA), online sexual harassment, gendertrolling, e-bile, disciplinary rhetoric; **Interactionist**; impact on inequality & identity, p60

Noveck et al. (2021): online community-building; **Weberian**; social media, virtual communities, impact on relationships, p36

Page (2019): *Perennials: the future of ageing*, perennials, nostalgia; **Weberian**; impact on identity, p57

Putnam (2000): *Bowling Alone*, social capital; **Functionalism**; social capital, p22

Ritzer (1993): *The McDonaldization of Society*, McDonaldisation, efficiency, calculability, predictability, control; **Weberian**; glocalisation, 51

Robinson (2004): transnational state, transnational bourgeoisie; **Marxist**; defining Globalisation, impact on inequality, conflict & change, p13

Ronson (2015): *So You've Been Publicly Shamed*, shaming; **Interactionist**; social media, virtual communities, impact on relationships, p35

Tufecki (2017): *Twitter & Tear Gas*, decentralised online movements, tactical freezes; **Post-Marxism**; impact on identity & equality, conflict & change, p53

FURTHER RESEARCH

These studies are less central to any argument. Some of them just reference a useful piece of terminology. Others offer criticism of a Key Study or are the original research that a Key Study is criticising.

Bates (2012): *Everyday Sexism Project*, p25

Baudrillard (1970): hyper-reality, simulacrum, p23

Bauman (2013): postmodern uncertainty, p41, 62

Bindel (2017): against sex-positivity, Gender Critical, p26

Bor & Peterson (2021): Mismatch Theory explains online conflict, p35

Bourdieu (1984): social reproduction not meritocracy, p57

Case (2007): supports **Haraway (1985)**, p55

Crenshaw (1991): intersectionality; p25

Duffy & Hewlett (2021): US culture wars exported to the UK, p47

Geraci et al. (2018): supports **Putnam (2000)**, p22

Livingstone (2018): transphobia on Mumsnet, p54

Lyotard (1979): death of meta-narratives, p23, 41

McIntosh (1988): white privilege, p52

Morozov (2011): slacktivism, p53

Postman (1994): *The Disappearance of Childhood*, p55

Turkle (2011): *Alone Together*, p62

Yee (2006): survey of relationships on *World of Warcraft*, p36

CRIME & DEVIANCE: CONTENT

What's this topic about?

This introduces you to the main sociological theories about Crime, in particular why crime occurs, what can be done about it and how it should be defined and measured.

This should help you answer some important questions:

- What is Crime in society: is it a terrible threat to the social order, a necessary evil or something that has been exaggerated to demonise certain unpopular social groups?

- Why is there Crime and Deviance: is it natural for people to break the rules or are they driven to do it by problems in society itself?

- What should be done about Crime: are criminals misunderstood and in need of help and rehabilitation? or are they dangers to society who need to be punished and locked away? Can we reduce crime by monitoring everybody closely or do we need instead to build a fairer society where crime isn't necessary?

Deviance

Deviance is behaviour that goes against social **norms**, leading to reactions like shock, outrage, disgust or fear. People feel strongly about deviance and deviant people are often condemned, tormented and outcast. However, deviance varies from culture to culture and time to time. This suggests it is, at least to some extent, **socially constructed** (p83). Deviant behaviour can involve taking drugs, dressing inappropriately, using forbidden language or disrespecting people or institutions that society considers important.

A lot of behaviour that used to be considered deviant is fairly normative now. For example, homosexuality, drug taking and wearing casual/revealing clothes used to be viewed very negatively but attitudes are changing. Deviance tends to bring on **informal social control**.

Crime is behaviour that goes against the written laws of the country and carries **formal sanctions**. It is a subject of **formal social control**. A lot of laws involve property, such as theft and trespass and vandalism. Laws are always being created and abolished and they also vary between countries and times. Homosexuality used to be illegal as did being a witch, but those things are no longer crimes in Western countries.

Many things are both criminal *and* deviant, such as murder and rape. Some things are *criminal but not particularly deviant*: the law will punish you for speeding or parking where you shouldn't, but your friends and workmates won't think worse of you for it. Other things are *deviant but not criminal*: it causes shock and outrage when someone cheats on their husband or wife but in Western countries the police won't get involved (even if the cheated person wishes they would).

CHAPTER 5 – MEASURING CRIME & DEVIANCE

This first part of the course is called *'How are crime and deviance defined and measured?'* so the first task is to think about some definitions. This is done through the broad Perspectives of Consensus, Conflict and Social Action introduced earlier in the A-Level.

SOCIAL ORDER & CONTROL

Social control is the way that society gets people to conform. This is done through the **agencies of social control** covered **in 1A: Socialisation, Culture & Identity**. These agencies can be **formal** (like the police and the courts) or **informal** (like families and peer groups).

Social order refers to the organisation of society around its beliefs: who holds power, who gets to define what is normal and what is deviant, what the formal agencies of social control are and what power they have, what happens to the deviants who break the rules?

The philosopher **Thomas Hobbes (1651)** answers this by describing a **social contract**. The contract is a metaphor (nobody literally signs a contract) for the sort of 'deal' we enter into with society: we give up certain freedoms to do as we please and in return society protects us and gives us the opportunity to study, earn and spend money and enjoy culture.

Consensus View of Social Order & Control

Émile Durkheim (1893) claims social order is based on shared values. It's a 'ground up' view that people naturally generate social order from their daily interactions – from their **culture**. This creates **social solidarity** which is a feeling of belonging. The people brought together by this experience a **collective conscience** – a shared sense of right and wrong and the meaning of life.

Durkheim contrasts **'mechanical solidarity'** of traditional pre-modern societies with the **'organic solidarity'** of modern societies. Mechanical solidarity exists when everybody does the same work (farming or hunting). Organic solidarity is when everybody is different from their neighbour (doing different jobs, different religions, etc) but they are all **interdependent**: they rely on each other to fulfil different roles and functions like different organs in the body.

This is a **Functionalist** view (p119). It proposes that the police act on our behalf and exert social control with our consent. Criminals break the social solidarity of the community and they need to be stopped and brought back into line to preserve social order. Social control is an expression of the community's values: our disapproval of crime and outrage at deviancy.

Conflict View of Social Order & Control

Karl Marx (1858) argues that social order is based on the economic structure of society. There are two components to society: the **base** (resources and the technology to exploit them) and the **superstructure** (institutions like government, churches, schools and families).

Marx argues that the superstructure grows out of the base and reflects the values of the **ruling class** that controls the base. The superstructure justifies the power of the ruling class. The base and the superstructure create and maintain social order together.

In **Capitalism**, this leads to a tiny ruling class dominating a huge working class. Social order is all about keeping this arrangement going and social control is used to stop anyone from threatening this arrangement.

This is a **Marxist** view (p125) but a similar argument is made by **Feminists** (p130), that social order consists of making half the population (women) subordinate to the other half and social control is used to keep women in line by justifying the inequality – or by threats and violence when women don't conform.

This view proposes that the police are acting on behalf of the ruling class in society. Criminals are threatening the wealth and power of the ruling group and they need to be stopped and brought back into line. Punishments are an expression of the **ruling class ideology**, and the fear of crime makes people consent to social control even though it isn't in their interests.

Social Action View of Social Order & Control

The Consensus and Conflict Perspectives are both **structuralist** views: neither of them recognises that individuals have agency or input into how society works and they propose that big institutions or impersonal economic forces are really in charge. They are **macro perspectives** viewing things on a society-wide scale.

Max Weber (1922) developed an **Interactionist** (p131) and **micro perspective**, which takes into account individual agency as well as powerful institutions. It is called a Social Action Perspective because it takes into account how society controls us but also how we can act to influence society.

Weber thinks **social actions** are of four types:

- **Traditional:** this involves following laws and customs because 'that's how it's always been done' and a lot of social order comes from this; it is similar to the Consensus and Conflict Perspectives
- **Affective:** this involves acting on feelings without thinking; both Consensus and Conflict Perspectives underestimate emotions
- **Value-Rational:** this is acting on your conscious beliefs, often the result of socialisation (e.g. believing in a religion); Consensus sees this as healthy for society but Conflict sees it as ruling class ideology at work
- **Instrumental-Rational:** acting deliberately in order to bring about changes in society; this is something Consensus and Conflict both underestimate

This view proposes that social order is shaped by traditions or powerful institutions (as Durkheim would agree) and these institutions support the wealthy and the powerful (as Marx would agree) – but ordinary people exert influence and can shape the way they are policed and controlled.

AO2 ILLUSTRATION: BLACK LIVES MATTER

Black Lives Matter (BLM) is a protest movement that started in 2012 when a Black high school student **Trayvon Martin** was shot and killed by an armed neighbourhood watchman who was later found not guilty of murder. In 2013, #BLM became a popular hashtag for online activism (*c.f.* **Section A**, p27). In 2014, the shooting of another Black American, **Michael Brown**, triggered weeks of protests against police violence in Ferguson, Missouri. More recently, the murder of **George Floyd** by a White police officer in 2020 prompted worldwide protests against racism and police brutality.

The BLM movement is de-centralised with no formal leadership or structure. A lot of activists speaking under the BLM banner call for defunding the police but also for feminism and LGBT rights, immigration reform and Social Justice.

In 2016, American football player **Colin Kaepernick 'took the knee'** instead of standing for the National Anthem, as a protest against racism and police brutality. The gesture has been widely adopted outside of sports, especially by the BLM movement.

Functionalists tend to defend the police by claiming they use proportionate force in a dangerous job (they take National Anthems quite seriously too). From a **Conflict Perspective**, the police serve the interests of the (White) ruling class and oppressing Black working class people is part of how they maintain social order. However, a **Social Action** Perspective shows how a **party** (the BLM movement) and individuals with **status** (Colin Kaepernick) can win public support and possibly bring about a change in social order and control.

Research: the Black Lives Matter movement and debates about 'taking the knee'

THE RELATIVITY OF CRIME & DEVIANCE

Crime and deviance are relative concepts. That means that what is defined as criminal or deviant is relative to the society where it happens or the Identity of the person doing it. Or to put it plainly, there's no absolute definition of what is or what isn't a crime or a deviant act and societies as well as onlookers make different distinctions.

For example, in Muslim-majority countries, drinking alcohol might be considered deviant or actually illegal. Gun ownership is legal in the USA but the exact laws regarding what guns can be owned and carried in public varies from State to State. As noted in **1A: Socialisation, Culture & Identity**, the age of majority (the age at which young people are considered adults) varies from country to country, so it's legal to sell alcohol to a 18-year-old in the UK but this is a crime in the USA. The rights of women, their access to education and what they can wear in public without being criticised or even arrested varies from country to country.

There is also **selective policing** (p92) where people from marginalised backgrounds are more likely to be viewed as 'acting suspiciously' and classed as committing a crime.

Consensus View of Relativity

The Consensus Perspective sees social order arising out of culture, so where cultures differ around the world you would expect the definitions of crime and deviance to vary too. However, alongside the variation, there's a lot of consistency too. Societies vary in how they punish crimes like murder and the things that might justify killing someone (such a defending your home or your family's honour) but they all have a crime called 'murder.'

Functionalists claim that culture ultimately reflects human biology: we are animals with physiological needs. **Talcott Parsons (1951)** argues there are functional prerequisites that a society has to meet in order for people to flourish. These include **adaptation to the environment** (providing people with food and shelter) and **pattern maintenance** (educating the next generation and passing on culture to them).

This means there are limits to how wildly societies can differ from each other. A society that bans having children or that makes it illegal to sell food will soon die out (and only the lawbreakers will survive).

Functionalists often believe that Western democracies with a Capitalist economy are the most advanced and successful because they best reflect our biological needs. This is the **'March of Progress.'** This belief leads to the idea that Western ideas of crime and deviance – especially the concept of human rights – should be exported to other countries so they can benefit from them too. As human rights become accepted round the world, crime and deviance become less relative – they are judged by a universal standard.

Research: revisit your notes on Globalisation (p7) and Cultural Homogenisation (p48) from **Section A**; the exporting of human rights is another aspect of Global Culture

Conflict View of Relativity

The Conflict Perspective sees social order being imposed to suit the interests of a ruling class. Different societies around the world will have a different economic base (some will be industrialised, some agricultural, some rich in oil or rare minerals) and this means their superstructure of institutions and culture will develop differently. This explains a lot of variation in ideas about crime and deviance.

Some societies might not have a Capitalist system in place and so don't have a tiny ruling class exploiting everyone else. This would lead to very different ideas about crime and deviance.

However, Capitalism has gone global. This means that **Marxists** end up agreeing with Functionalists that societies don't vary too much, although for different reasons.

Marxists are interested in **selective policing** (p92). The power of ruling class ideology means that bystanders are more likely to report the behaviour of people who are working class or Black as 'suspicious' and the police are more likely to arrest (or, in the USA, shoot) suspects from marginalised groups.

Feminists similarly think that Patriarchy is a worldwide problem. Different societies are relatively safe or relatively dangerous for women, but they all subordinate women to men in some sense. Violence against women is a worldwide problem and one which all societies tend to ignore or justify. Moreover, Feminists accuse the police of not taking violence against women as seriously as violence against other men.

Research: revisit your notes on the 'transnational bourgeoisie' (p13) from **Section A** and link crime and deviance to a Networked Global Society (p30).

Social Action View of Relativity

Differing definitions of crime and deviance are easily explained by the Social Action Perspective, which recognises that ordinary people – especially when united by a movement and emboldened by strong beliefs – can reshape the society around them.

Max Weber (1905) links the invention of Capitalism itself to the '***Protestant work ethic.***' He proposes that a group of European Christians (Protestants) developed a belief that God commanded hard work and unselfishness but revealed his blessing through success in business. This motivated people to work hard to earn money, but instead of spending the money on luxuries or religious monuments they re-invested the profits back into their businesses.

Weber's point is that a relatively small number of people can reshape society in unexpected ways if they have strong beliefs. This is similar to the Marxist view that the spread of Capitalism will create similarities in crime and deviance everywhere, but Social Action claims different societies will have different reactions to Capitalism, based on their beliefs. Beliefs also affect how police deal with crime, especially why some people are targeted by the police with greater force.

AO2 ILLUSTRATION: BLACK LIVES MATTER continued

The **Black Lives Matter** movement was prompted by the killings of Black Americans by the police – and specifically White police officers. Here are some tragic examples:

17-year-old **Trayvon Martin** was shot in 2012 by a White neighbourhood watch volunteer armed with a 9mm semi-automatic pistol. The killer was arrested but acquitted, because it could not be proved he hadn't been acting in self-defence.

In 2014, **Michael Brown** (18) was walking with a friend when they were stopped by a police officer. The officer shot and killed Brown but claimed self-defence and was not charged.

In 2018, **Stephon Clark** (22) was shot more than 20 times while standing in his grandmother's yard. They believed he was holding a gun but it was a mobile phone. No officers were charged with his death.

In 2020, **Breona Taylor** (26) and her boyfriend were asleep when plainclothes police officers broke into their house looking for drugs. Shots were fired and Taylor was killed. None of the officers were charged for Taylor's death.

Also in 2020, **George Floyd** was arrested walking home from a convenience store. The police officer Derek Chauvin knelt on Floyd's neck for 9 minutes 26 seconds, despite Floyd repeatedly telling officers he could not breathe before he died. The incident was filmed by bystanders. Chauvin was convicted of murder.

Black Lives Matter claim that Black Americans are stopped more often than White citizens and are more likely to be killed by police violence. This illustrates **relativity** because the same behaviour carried out by a White or a Black person gets different responses from the police, with the Black person more likely to be challenged and dealt with violently.

Black Lives Matter – We Won't Be Silenced (photo: alisdare21)

SOCIAL CONSTRUCTION OF CRIME & DEVIANCE

Social construction is the way that human interpretations shaped by cultural and historical contexts create characteristic that are typically thought to be objective and biological—such as gender, race, class and sexuality (**Subramaniam, 2010**).

All sociologists are 'soft' social contructivists, because they admit that social attitudes play a part in shaping what counts as a crime or a deviant act – this is the basis for the **relativism of crime and deviance**.

Some sociologists are 'hard' social constructivists who go further than this and argue that criminal and deviant acts are *entirely* a product of social attitudes: society creates crime and crime wouldn't exist if it wasn't for social attitudes.

Consensus View of Social Construction

Functionalists assume that biology shapes society to some extent. This means they think that crime is inevitable, given that we are competitive animals and there will never be a perfect match between the culture we create and our biological limitations.

Émile Durkheim (1895) explains this by imagining the **'society of saints'** where everyone is an *"exemplary individual"* and *"crimes are unknown."* Durkheim argues that there will still be *"faults"* among the saints. These faults appear trivial to outsiders (perhaps, forgetting to say 'Bless You' when someone sneezes) but among the saints they cause *"the same scandal that the ordinary offense does in ordinary consciousness."* This illustrates both the **relativity** of deviance and the way it is **socially constructed**.

Despite this, Functionalists believe crime is real: criminal activities actually happen and are not entirely in the imagination of newspapers and governments. This understanding informs the **Right Realist** Perspective (p123).

Conflict View of Social Construction

Traditional **Marxists** tend towards 'hard' social constructivism when it comes to crime. They propose that most crime is really a fiction created by police reports, government statistics and news stories to demonise marginalised groups (especially the working class) and spread fear. The Capitalist class is then able to justify heavy-handed policing to deal with a non-existent problem. Meanwhile **white collar crime** is barely reported or policed.

The story of Marxist criminology is one of gradually surrendering this position in favour of a 'soft' constructivist one. **Neo-Marxists** in the 1970s admit that working class crime exists (p126) and **Left Realism** in the 1980s and '90s acknowledges the need to be tough on crime as well as the causes of crime (p128).

Feminists identify the opposite problem: crimes against women are downplayed rather than exaggerated and it's common to 'blame the victim' for the way she acted or dressed. This 'soft' social construction of crimes against women makes women responsible for their own victimisation and justifies male criminals for acting out of 'provocation' or a 'misunderstanding.'

Social Action View of Social Construction

The Social Action Perspective promotes the concept of 'hard' Social Construction. **Howard Becker** developed a type of Interactionism called **Labelling Theory** in his book *Outsiders* (1963). Becker suggests that our interactions with others causes us to pick up 'labels' that affect how other people view us and therefore how future interactions work out. Some people are given **deviant labels** (e.g. 'thief' or 'promiscuous'). Over time, we can **internalise** labels and believe they are part of our Identity: this is the **Self-Fulfilling Prophecy (SFP)**. Some labels have **Master Status** and overrule all other labels.

Becker defines the process like this: *"social groups create deviance by making rules whose infraction creates deviance, and by applying those rules to particular people and labelling them as outsiders."*

This means that society interprets the behaviour of people with the 'deviant' label as deviant, even if it is entirely innocent (and, indeed, no different from other behaviour going on all around) – and interprets the behaviour of 'respectable' people as non-deviant even when they behave in exactly the same way.

If you remember being punished by a teacher for something the rest of the class was doing too you will have a lot of sympathy with this theory.

AO2 ILLUSTRATION: SLUTWALKS

In 2011, a Canadian police officer suggested *"women should avoid dressing like sluts"* if they want to avoid sexual assault. There was a Feminist outcry against this type of victim-blaming. The protest took the form of a **SlutWalk**, a march where women dressed in a way considered to be 'slutty' such as short skirts, stockings and scanty tops, asserting their freedom to dress how they wish and right to be protected by the law when so doing. The organisers expected 200 people to take part in Toronto but 3000 participated.

SlutWalk NYC October 2011 (photo: David_shankbone)

Similar SlutWalks have taken place in cities worldwide. Feminist **Jessica Valenti (2011)** says: *"SlutWalks have become the most successful feminist action of the past 20 years."*

SlutWalks are also part of the #MeToo movement and **4th Wave Feminism**, in particular its **sex-positive** attitude (*c.f.* **Section A**). They draw attention to the **socially constructed** nature of sexual crimes against women, since women's clothing is viewed as provoking (and excusing) assaults. They also point out the **relativism of crime**, since assaults against men are not treated less seriously based on how men are dressed. According to **Valenti (2011)**: *"The idea that women's clothing has some bearing on whether they will be raped is a dangerous myth feminists have tried to debunk for decades."*

RESEARCH PROFILE: PEARSON (1983)

Geoffrey Pearson wrote *Hooligan: A history of respectable fears* (1983) after observing reactions to the riots in Brixton (London) and other British cities. Pearson noted the way Right Wing commentators blamed poorly socialised youths and single parent families for the riots and wrote this book as a response.

The attitudes Pearson is addressing are those of the **New Right**, *which emerged at this time.*

Pearson shows how concerns about aimless and violent youths are nothing new. He gives a detailed analysis of the **Teddy Boy Subculture** of the 1950s, which shocked post-War Britain with gang fighting and vandalism. He reports how punishments were toughened up to deal with these delinquents, including the first **'short sharp shock'** Detention Centres (p68) and the Youth Training Scheme to get school-leavers into jobs (similar to later views by the **New Right**, p50).

Pearson shows that the 'Teds' appeared before televisions were widely owned, rock & roll music had crossed over from America or wartime meat rationing had ended, so they were not the result of bad influences from TV, America or having too much comfort.

Instead, Pearson shows that these youth gangs were nothing new and British society has *always* had these fears about delinquency. He compares the Teds to the original Edwardian delinquents known as 'Muggers' or 'Hooligans' and details the fighting, street crime and assaults on police from the hot summer of 1868. A generation earlier, the 'Garrotters' of caused concern in Victorian Britain and the trend goes back to the 'unruly apprentices' of the Middle Ages.

Pearson's point is that youth deviance and crime has always been with us but is often presented as something new and used to justify a crackdown on working class people and criticism of their families and lifestyles. This is a **Marxist** view that shows that apparent crime waves can be **socially constructed** and only **relative** to other periods in history. However, it also resembles **Durkheim**'s argument that crime and deviance are inevitable (p12).

Research: if you studied Youth Deviance and Moral Panics for **1B: Youth Subcultures** then Pearson's work makes an excellent study for those topics too.

MEASURING CRIME & DEVIANCE: A TOOLKIT

It is important to measure crime in order to identify trends: is a particular type of crime becoming more common or less common? It's essential to know this to work out how to deploy police resources and to calculate whether crime prevention strategies are working.

The Dark Figure

Clive Hollin (1989) points out a major problem with criminology which he calls '**the Dark Figure of unrecorded crime.**' This is the idea that **most crime goes unrecorded** – Hollin suggests only 25% of crime makes it into the recorded figures. The Dark Figure is partly a result of crimes being reported but not recorded (e.g. because the police don't take them seriously). Some crimes are reported to other agencies (like insurance companies or schoolteachers) and dealt with at that level, without involving the law. There are crimes that people don't realise have happened to them, such as fraud. Sexual assaults fall into this category if the victims blame themselves and don't view the attack as a crime. It also includes victims who don't report crime out of shame or fear of reprisals or a distrust of the police.

Finally, there are so-called 'victimless' crimes that target business (like shoplifting) or other institutions (like tax evasion) and this includes crimes against the environment. Of course, there *are* victims of 'victimless' crimes (such as health problems from pollution or injuries from safety standards being ignored) but nobody feels *personally* targeted by them so there isn't a strong motive to report or investigate them.

RESEARCH PROFILE: MUMSNET (2012)

The social media site *Mumsnet* carried out a **Sexual Assault Survey** of 1609 users as part of their '*We Believe You*' campaign in 2012: 27% reported being raped and 52% sexually assaulted but 83% of those who experienced rape or sexual assault did *not* report it to the police, with one half saying this was because of shame and two thirds saying they would hesitate to report rape or sexual assault because they didn't expect their attacker to be convicted.

Mumsnet founder **Justine Roberts** blames "*the feeling among many women that they can't talk about these crimes for fear of being treated unsympathetically, denying them access to practical and emotional support when they need it most.*"

This is a **victim survey** (p89) with a **volunteer (self-selecting) sample**, so it's possible the results are influenced by respondents who had a bad experience of the justice system (and want to complain) but those who had a good experience (and who reported the crime) did not feel the need to respond to the survey.

Research: find out more about the 'We Believe You' survey; review your notes from **2A: Research Methods** on volunteer sampling

OFFICIAL CRIME STATISTICS (OCS)

Official crime statistics (OCS) are records kept by the government. They are used to track the rise and fall of crime nationally and regionally and are the figures that tend to get reported in the news. These statistics are collected every 6 months by the Home Office and published by the **Office for National Statistics (ONS)**.

Positive Views of Official Crime Statistics

Official statistics are quite up to date, cover the whole country and provide a **'whole count'** – they are not an estimate based on a sample. They consist of **quantitative data** which can be analysed statistically to get objective conclusions about **patterns and trends** in crime (p95).

These statistics are **standardised**, which means the different categories have a fixed meaning and relate to legal distinctions (e.g. different classes of illegal drugs). This standardisation means you can trace the statistics back over many years and detect the rise and fall of different types of crimes. This is essential for investigating whether **crime prevention strategies** are working (p135) and how crime rates relate to other changes in society (like unemployment increasing or decreasing) which is important for **explaining crime** (p117).

Negative Views of Official Crime Statistics

OCS suffers particularly badly from the **Dark Figure** of unrecorded crime because many people do not report crimes to the authorities. Some crimes are reported but to authorities other than the government: children might report a crime to parents or schoolteachers who deal with it without involving the police. Criminals tend to deal with crime themselves (leading to gang warfare) rather than involving the authorities. **Summary offences** (like motoring offences) don't get included in the figures. These gaps in the data make OCS **invalid**.

Although OCS are standardised, the categories used often change. Sometimes this is because the law changes (for example, a previously legal drug is criminalised, creating a lot more crimes when people continue using it) or categories are re-defined. This means it's not always possible to draw clear trends over time and it makes OCS **unreliable**.

Some crimes are reported more if a campaign has drawn public attention to the problem: this creates the false impression that the crime has become more common when it is merely being reported more often. This makes the data **invalid** and **unreliable**.

*If you studied **Moral Panics** for **1B** (options in **Youth Subcultures** or **Media**), you can apply your understanding of **deviancy amplification spirals** to this problem with OCS.*

OCS figures are quite simplistic. They do not gather rich data on the identity of the victim or the motives of the criminal – for that, you need a **victim survey** (p89) or a **self-report study** (p91).

AO2 ILLUSTRATION: CRIMES KNOWN TO THE POLICE (CKP)

There are 43 police forces in England & Wales, along with the British Transport Police and separate police forces in Scotland and Northern Ireland. Each police force keeps a record of reported crimes and submits this to the Home Office every 6 month to form a major part of OCS.

According to **John Lambert (1970)**, the problem with CKP lies in **police discretion**. Police officers have choice (discretion) over whether to arrest someone, issue a caution or a more informal warning. Warnings often aren't recorded and police discretion extends to what particular offence to arrest or caution someone for and what details to put in the final written report. This can make CKP a very **unreliable** measure of crime and particularly prone to **labelling** (p84), since the police often act with the concept of an **'ideal criminal'** in mind and are more likely to record as crimes behaviour by people meeting this **stereotype**.

This flaw with CKP is used to explain the over-representation of ethnic minorities (p105) in OCS.

Police forces are given political direction by the Home Office, which can include instructions to focus on particular crimes and focus less on others (for example, to concentrate on knife crimes but not on burglaries). This also skews CKP, showing an increase in some crimes and a decrease in others that isn't based on reality (**invalid**). **Feminists** accuse the police of not taking crimes against women seriously and being hostile and unbelieving when women report rape, leading to lower recording of these crimes.

Research: find out more about police discretion in the debate over 'Stop & Search'

RESEARCH PROFILE: HOLDAWAY (1980)

Simon Holdaway is a pioneer of police research. While he was a sergeant in the London Metropolitan Police in the 1970s, Holdaway conducted a ground-breaking (**covert**) **ethnographic** study of police work: *The Occupational Culture of Urban Policing*.

Holdaway argues that the police cannot deal with all offences so they have to prioritise. This leads to an **occupational culture** (like a **subculture**) which **socialises** officers into a set of unusual norms and values. **Police discretion** is at the centre of this culture and means 'turning a blind eye' when an offence is too minor or not worth the effort to follow up. The occupational culture values action and aggression, which leads to norms focusing on particular types of offences (e.g. violent crime) at the expense of less exciting crimes (e.g. traffic offences, shoplifting).

Holdaway also reports a culture of racism revealed by derogatory language, jokes and banter between White police officers in police stations.

Since it is based on his own experiences as well as interviews and observations with ordinary police officers, Holdaway's study carries a lot of authority (**validity**). However, policing has changed a lot since then, notably the Metropolitan Police being criticised by the **Macpherson Report** (p129) which led to an attempt to change the occupational culture.

VICTIM SURVEYS

Victim Surveys involve asking members of the public what crimes they have been a victim of in the past.

Positive Views of Victim Surveys

Victim surveys reveal the sort of crimes that people do not report to the police (or feel were ignored by the police), so they are very important for exploring the **Dark Figure** of unrecorded crime (p86).

Victim surveys also reveal **patterns of victimisation** that do not show up in police reports. For example, official statistics tend to show that women are unlikely to be victims of crime, but victim surveys allow women to report many more experiences of victimisation that they either do not report to the police or feel are not taken seriously by the police.

Like OCS, victim surveys are carried out on a **national level** but **local surveys** are also conducted, which shows the effect of crime at a neighbourhood level. They can be **standardised** just like OCS but they can gather more supplementary data than OCS, such as the victim's age, class, gender or ethnicity and their feelings of safety or trauma.

Negative Views of Victim Surveys

Victim surveys do not provide a 'whole count' – they are a **sample** of the total population and trends can only be **estimated** based on them. If the sample is unrepresentative then the data will be **unreliable**.

Many people approached to take part in a victim survey do not respond and it is possible that these are people with no experience of crime, meaning that the data is skewed to exaggerate victimisation. Some people are not included in victim surveys, such as people with no fixed address (homeless, migrants, etc) and children.

Since the survey is a written questionnaire, people with low levels of literacy might be intimidated by it and if they refuse to complete it (or complete it badly) then the results will not reflect their experiences. This tends to mean that victim surveys reflect the experiences of better-educated and more middle-class people.

There is also the possibility that victim surveys are answered untruthfully. Respondents might be too ashamed or traumatised to write about a crime. Alternatively, they might **exaggerate** the seriousness or frequency of crime in their life (perhaps in the hope that politicians will act on the results or simply because they have vivid imaginations).

Victim surveys do not gather data on 'victimless' crimes (such as shoplifting), crimes that are not detected by the victim (such as fraud) or crimes the victim doesn't interpret as crime (such as some sexual assaults).

AO2 ILLUSTRATION: CRIME SURVEY FOR ENGLAND & WALES

The British Crime Survey (BCS) began in 1982. After the Scottish Government introduced its own survey, the BCS became the **Crime Survey for England & Wales (CSEW)** in 2012.

The CSEW surveys 50,000 people aged 16+ every year but also conducts 4000 interviews with children aged 10-15. The results are published alongside CKP by the Office for National Statistics (ONS). It measures experiences of crime in the previous 12 months. The response rate is only 75%, which lowers the reliability of the data, especially if people with very high or very low experiences of crime are not responding. However, this is still quite a high response rate relative to many other surveys.

The CSEW **caps** the number of times a crime can be reported at 5. In other words, if you were mugged 7 times in the last year, this would be treated as 5 muggings. **Graham Farrell (2007)** estimates that the CSEW underestimates crime by 3 million offences a year because of this and this might particularly affect the reporting of domestic violence, which could be 140% higher. This cap has been **standardised** since the start of the BCS, so trends are **reliable** over time.

Research: visit the CSEW website on https://ukdataservice.ac.uk/

RESEARCH PROFILE: JONES, MACLEAN & YOUNG (1986)

A local victim survey that is very important in the history of sociology is the **Islington Crime Survey**, carried out by a research team from Middlesex University: **Trevor Jones**, **Brian Maclean** & **Jock Young**.

If you recognise Jock Young as a famous Neo-Marxist sociologist, well done!

Islington is a borough in North London that has always had high levels of deprivation. The team surveyed 2000 residents about their experience of crime (which was rising sharply at the time), their fear of crime and their attitudes to the police. Instead of just using a questionnaire, they carried out sympathetic unstructured interviews.

A third of respondents had experienced serious crime in the previous twelve months, such as sexual assault, domestic violence and racial attacks. A quarter avoided going out after dark because of fear of crime and 28% felt unsafe in their own homes. Women experienced a 'curfew' – over half the women in the sample never went out after dark because of their fear of crime.

These results were (and are) shocking. They caused Jones et al. to re-assess their **Radical Criminology** (p126) views and develop a new **Left Realist** position (p128) based on the insight that crime is real and the poorest people are the victims.

The use of **unstructured interviews** lowers the **reliability** of the study, even though it increases the willingness of the respondents to open up (**high validity**). A local survey like this cannot be generalised to other areas or to Islington today, over 30 years later.

SELF-REPORT STUDIES

Victim studies question the victims of crimes, but **self-report studies** question the criminals themselves. The simplest form of self-report study involves a questionnaire with a list of offences and the respondents tick off the offences they have committed (either ever committed or committed in the last year).

They're a bit like those 'Never Have I Ever …?' memes that circulate online.

NEVER HAVE I EVER

GIVE YOURSELF 1 POINT FOR EACH THING YOU HAVEN'T DONE

1. Skipped school
2. Broken a bone
3. Fired a gun
4. Done drugs
5. Been in a limo
6. Gotten a tattoo
7. Ridden a horse
8. Sung karaoke
9. Gotten a ticket
10. Been arrested
11. Gone zip lining
12. Been on TV
13. Been on a cruise
14. Gotten a peircing
15. Smoked
16. Met a celeb
17. Been skydiving
18. Had a 1 night stand
19. Skinny dipped
20. Been drunk

This one went viral on Twitter in 2020

Positive Views of Self-Report Studies

Self-report studies are an effective way to explore the **Dark Figure** of unrecorded crime (p86), because the offenders know what they have done, even if they got away with it undetected. They challenge stereotypes about the **'ideal criminal'** since they often reveal the extent of female criminality and middle-class criminality to be much higher than OCS suggest.

Self-report studies are often **longitudinal**, getting the same cohort to repeat the questionnaire every year. This provides valuable data about how criminal behaviour changes with age or in response to changes in the law or new policing strategies.

Negative Views of Self-Report Studies

There are huge problems with getting people to self-report the crimes they have committed. People who have committed serious crimes will not confess to them on a questionnaire. Even if they did, this would create an **ethical problem** for the researchers, who would then have to report the crime to the police or else become 'accessories after the fact' (because they are helping to conceal a crime).

Because of this, most self-report studies are of teenager cohorts and focus on **delinquency** and minor crimes. However, these are a type of offending that is often missed out by OCS since many people don't think it's worth reporting and police often respond with informal warnings.

AO2 ILLUSTRATION: SELECTIVE POLICING

One of the main findings to come out of self-report surveys is that the stereotype of the 'ideal criminal' might not be based in reality. Various self-report studies suggest that 50-90% of the population admit to behaviour which could get them arrested.

In particular, the difference in offences reported by working-class and middle-class people isn't as great as is thought (**Martin Gold, 1966**, found it a working-class-to-middle-class ratio of 1.5:1) and the offending of women is closer to men that is assumed (**Anne Campbell, 1981**, found a male-to-female ratio of 1.3:1). However, both of these were self-report studies of delinquents, not adult criminals.

Steven Box (1983) suggests that this data indicates the flaws in a **selective approach to law enforcement**, with the police targeting some groups based on preconceived ideas rather than the actual likelihood of their offending.

This might explain the perception that Black drivers are disproportionately stopped by the police. This was reported by the British athlete **Bianca Williams** and the Labour MP **Dawn Butler** in 2020. Also in 2020, a video went viral of a driver in Ely, Cambridgeshire being stopped by police who told him: *"The reason I've stopped you is … – no offence to you, but you're a black male, OK, I'm not going to lie to you."*

Stop & Search (photos: Darren Johnson/iDJ Photography)

Research: find out more about **Stop & Search** and the cases mentioned above

RESEARCH PROFILE: SHAW (1930)

It's an old book, but **Clifford Shaw**'s *The Jack Roller* (1930) is an absolute classic in criminology. It's a self-report study of a Chicago delinquent named **Stanley**, between the ages 16-22. Stanley was interviewed by Shaw and contributed a 250-page description of his life; Shaw also obtained police and court papers to back up what Stanley told him.

Stanley starts stealing before he starts school, is a persistent truant and graduates in his teens to burglary and "Jack Rolling" (a slang term for robbing drunks and homosexual men who proposition him). He spends time in Detention Centres.

Stanley blames **external factors** for his offending: "*To start out in life, everyone has his chances—some good and some very bad … My start was handicapped by a no-good, ignorant, and selfish stepmother, who thought only of herself and her own children.*" Stanley's stepmother encourages him to steal but it is also a "*neighbourhood tradition*" in the deprived area where he grows up. Stanley runs away from home at age 6 to live on the streets, which he finds exciting and liberating.

Stanley also has an impulsive and thrill-seeking personality: "*How I loved to do these things! They thrilled me.*" However, he also picks up a criminal 'code' from the older boys and men he meets, which is **secondary socialisation by peers** into a **deviant subculture**. The strict discipline in reform schools only hardens him: "*I rebelled and harbored vengeance and hate.*"

At age 16, after leaving the Chicago House of Correction (prison), Stanley has a turning point. Shaw arranges for him to be fostered by a loving family; Stanley breaks off contact with his criminal friends, educates himself and finds a career; later he marries.

Jon Snodgrass (1972) tracked down Stanley before he died at age 75 and learned what became of him. Stanley lost his job in the Depression, divorced, returned to crime and spent time in a mental institution, but later remarried and retired. Stanley sums up his life saying: "*I would like to dwell on how fortunate I am to have lived through the early traumatic years and yet to have emerged relatively unscathed … I shall always remember, however, the humble days of adversity, living in the shadow of the horn of plenty.*"

Stanley's phrase 'living in the shadow of the horn of plenty' (a mythological symbol of wealth) links to **Philippe Bourgois (1995)** describing teenage crack-dealers in New York: "*the anguish of growing up poor in the richest city in the world*" and the idea of **relative deprivation** (p128).

Shaw's study is entirely **qualitative** data, using an **Interpretivist** methodology to explore the meaning of an offender's choices and circumstances. It is from a **Social Action** Perspective, with a focus on Stanley's freewill.

Research: find out more about the Jack Roller and Stanley's life; if you studied the **Youth Subculture**s option for **1B**, add this study to your notes on Interactionist explanations of youth deviance

EXAM PRACTICE: MEASURING CRIME & DEVIANCE

The OCR exam has three questions in **Paper 3 Section B**. Questions 7-9 are on Education and questions 10-12 are on Religion, Belief & Faith, but this Study Guide is focused on **Option 1** which covers questions **4-6**:

4. In what ways are crime and deviance relative? **[10 marks: 6 AO1 + 4 AO2]**

This is one of those 'describe & illustrate' questions, but with no Source A or Source B to lean on. No need to evaluate.

*Make **two** sociological points about relativism – perhaps from a Consensus and a Conflict viewpoint. It's a good idea to refer to named sociologists (like Durkheim, Marx, Weber, Pearson's **Hooligans** etc.) and you should definitely use some sociological terminology (like social solidarity, socialisation, ideology, superstructure). Then offer brief examples of relativism and make sure each example has an explanation of **why** it is relative. For example, "Stop & Search targets black drivers when the police view them as more likely not be criminals relative to white drivers."*

5. To what extent are official crime statistics trustworthy? **[20 marks: 8 AO1 + 4 AO2 + 8 AO3]**

This is a mid-size essay with a requirement for developed evaluation. You should spend 25 minutes and write at least 500 words.

*Write **three** points. Each point should introduce a sociological idea with some brief illustration from the real world. Each point should finish off with a developed evaluation (see **Chapter 9** for this). For example, you could write about OCS being standardised, the Dark Figure of unrecorded crime and the problem of police discretion. Make sure you mention **Holdaway**'s study on occupational culture in policing and be sure to answer the question: are OCS trustworthy or not?*

6. Outline and evaluate the problems in measuring crime effectively. **[40 marks: 16 AO1 + 8 AO2 + 16 AO3]**

This is the last of the two big (40 mark) essays in OCR A-Level Sociology. You should spend 50 minutes and write at least 1000 words.

*Write **four** points. Each point should introduce a sociological idea with some illustration from the real world. Each point should finish off with a developed evaluation (see **Chapter 9** for this). For example, you could write about the Dark Figure of unrecorded crime, then about OCS, victim surveys and self-report surveys and then finish with either the problem of police discretion or selective policing. Be sure to come to a conclusion: can we or can we not measure crime effectively?*

CHAPTER 6 – PATTERNS & TRENDS IN CRIME

The idea of patterns and trends in crime is clearly linked to **measuring crime**. It's hard to write about one without bringing in the other. It's also linked to **theoretical explanations of crime** (p117) which offer reasons for these patterns and trends. It's a good idea to use these other ideas to evaluate patterns and trends in your essays. For example, if you write about a trend, you could evaluate it by explaining the problems of relying on **official crime statistics** (p87) or how this trend backs up or disproves a **Left Realist** explanation (p128). All patterns and trends can be criticised by bringing in the **Dark Figure** of unrecorded crime (p86).

*Some of the research from **Chapter 5** fits into this chapter too; for example, **Pearson**'s study of Hooligans shows trends over the centuries, **self-report studies** show patterns that are not in line with stereotypes and the **Islington Crime Survey** (p90) revealed surprising things about patterns of victimisation.*

The Great Crime Decline

After the Second World War, the UK and the USA were relatively law-abiding societies. However, from the 1950s to the 1970s crime rates increased steadily and reached an all-time high in the 1980s. There were fears that some American cities were becoming no-go areas and British inner cities had become dangerous places compared to previous decades.

In the USA, handgun-related homicides more than doubled between 1985-1990 and in 1990 there were a record 2245 murders in New York city alone.

Strangely, crime rates then started dropping. By 2000, the homicide rate in the USA had almost halved, violent crime dropped by a third and murders in New York went down by 75%.

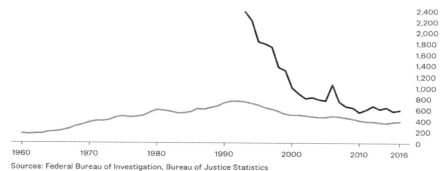

Sources: Federal Bureau of Investigation, Bureau of Justice Statistics
Does not include simple assaults where no weapon was used or no serious injury resulted.

Violent crime in the USA (per 100,000 population)

Something similar occurred in the UK, with crime rising throughout the 20th century and doubling in the 1960s, with an average of a million crimes reported each year, rising to 2 million in the 1970s and 3.5 million in the 1980s. Recorded offences reached 6 million in 2003 but have been dropping ever since (source: **Thompson et al., 2012**). The CSEW reports victimisation peaking earlier, in 1995, and dropping after that down to pre-1980s levels.

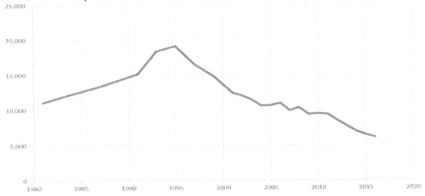

Crime in England and Wales from the CSEW (in 1000s of crimes)

The fall in crime is particularly surprising because it continued *after* the **Global Financial Crisis (GFC)** of **2008** which closed business and froze wages for many other people.

Criminologists are divided over the reasons for the Decline. Is it new technology like CCTV making crime more difficult (p138) or the Internet offering entertaining alternatives to crime? Is it tough **zero tolerance policing** (p140), **target hardening** (p137) or **welfare tackling poverty** (p147)? Or is it a reduction of lead in the air we breathe because of unleaded petrol in cars? Or (controversially) has the legalisation of abortion resulted in fewer unwanted children being born who would otherwise grow up to be criminals?

RESEARCH PROFILE: SHARKEY (2018)

Patrick Sharkey (2018) terms this drop in crime *"the Great Crime Decline"* and describes the period from the 1990s to today as an *"**Uneasy Peace**"* (the title of his book).

Sharkey links the Decline in the USA to tough policing and incarceration policies (currently the USA imprisons 0.7% of its population, which is a huge proportion, compared to 0.09% in the UK). He argues that although these policies have made deprived neighbourhoods safer, they also produce resentment and risk a backlash, which is why the peace is *"uneasy."*

Sharkey predicts the Decline will soon end. In 2020, in the middle of the 2020-22 Coronavirus Epidemic, the USA recorded the highest number of gun deaths in its history, which might be a sign of this happening.

*You could link this theory to **Shaw**'s study of Stanley (p93) who "harboured vengeance and hate" because of the strict discipline in reform schools – and also **Zero Tolerance Policing** (p140)*

PERSPECTIVES ON PATTERNS & TRENDS

Views on the meaning of patterns and trends vary from Perspective to Perspective but all have to grapple with the implications of the **Great Crime Decline** (p95).

CONSENSUS PERSPECTIVE: FUNCTIONALISM & NEW RIGHT

Functionalism places great faith in official statistics (it has a **positivist** view of research methods) and regards the patterns and trends revealed in statistics as **social facts** – direct insights into what is taking place in society. They do so even though the **Dark Figure** of unrecorded crime exists (p86) because they don't regard this unknown figure as changing the overall picture.

Functionalists take the **Great Crime Decline** at face value and link it to **progress** in society: better law enforcement, better standards of living, Capitalism ironing out its problems.

However, Functionalists have a complex relationship with crime. They regard crime as **inevitable** in society (p83) and as an indicator of **dysfunction**. If there is social dysfunction then crime will rise– and Functionalists believe there *is* dysfunction, such as high divorce rates and **strain** over available opportunities (p120). The **New Right** goes further than this, arguing that society is fundamentally broken by over-generous welfare and an **Underclass** producing delinquency and petty crime (p122). Because of this, there *ought* to be increasing crime, not decreasing crime. The New Right focuses on trends linked to badly socialised youth, like **knife crime** (p109), and Functionalists focus on drug crimes and **'yobbish' behaviour**. They often claim that these crimes are 'swept under the carpet' by the police, with the reality on the streets being worse than it appears in statistics.

This puts the Consensus Perspective in the odd position of celebrating the decline of crime, while at the same time arguing that the important types of crime are increasing – and of claiming crime patterns and trends are social facts while insisting some of them are **socially constructed** (p83).

RESEARCH PROFILE: FALK ET AL. (2013)

Orjan Falk et al. (2013) carried out a study in Sweden and concluded that the majority of all violent crime is committed by a small number of people. They are almost all **male** (92%) with **substance abuse problems**, often **diagnosed with personality disorders**. The researchers examined 2.5 million people in Swedish criminal and population records between 1973-2004. They found that 4% were convicted of at least one violent crime, and 26% were re-convicted 3+ times; this leads to the conclusion that **1% of the population accounts for 63% of all violent crime convictions** during the period being studied.

This supports the Consensus view of a hard core of antisocial deviants driving up the worst crime figures. However, the results are only representative of Sweden in the 1973-2004 period and only account for convicted offenders; it ignores the Dark Figure of unrecorded crime and offenders who were not convicted (e.g. due to lack of evidence).

CONFLICT PERSPECTIVE: MARXISM & NEO-MARXISM

Marxism usually places great faith in statistics (especially to reveal **Inequality**) but abandons this positivist view when it comes to crime. Traditional Marxists regarded **official crime statistics** (p87) as a piece of fiction and crime reporting in the news to be propaganda. For them, the working classes are innocent, and the real criminals are the ruling classes.

Because Capitalism is **criminogenic** (creates crime because of its injustices) there ought to be lots of unreported crime: **white collar crime**, **corporate crime** (by businesses) and **state crime**.

Therefore, most Marxists are sceptical about the **Great Crime Decline** (p95) and the idea that Capitalism has 'fixed' itself.

Neo-Marxists have a rather more complicated view of patterns and trends in crime. **The Radical Criminology** school (p126) and **Left Realism** (p128) both accept that the statistics *do* reflect working-class crime. However, they contend that the media leads **moral panics** (p101) to exaggerate the extent of this sort of crime and also to exaggerate Black crime. This is done to distract attention from economic problems in Capitalism and increase the fear of crime.

This means that **Neo-Marxists** are in the position of arguing that the **Great Crime Decline** is real and linking it to their successful policies (a Democrat President governed the USA in the 1990s and a Labour government came into power in the UK in 1997 through to 2010) while at the same time arguing that the statistics for crime are untrustworthy and exaggerated.

RESEARCH PROFILE: HALL (1978)

Stuart Hall is a **Neo-Marxist** who wrote *Policing The Crisis* (**1978**) at a time when the UK was rocked by strikes and suffering mass unemployment. Hall uses statistics to show that the fear of 'mugging' was unreasonable as the crime had gone *down* since the 1960s, not up, and was more likely to be carried out by White criminals. Hall points out that the British newspapers started a **moral panic** (p101) about **Black muggers** at a time when there was a genuine chance of Capitalism collapsing. This distracted people from the crisis, inflamed hostility between the White and Black working classes and justified police crackdowns.

This is termed the **'divide & rule'** approach to **social control** (p77): making marginalised groups (the White and Black working classes) hostile to each other so they never unite to challenge hegemonic power. The White working class welcome the deployment of heavy policing, because they believe (wrongly) it is protecting them.

Hall has been criticised for proposing a **conspiracy theory** without demonstrating exactly *how* the government and the newspaper editors organise to spread this false narrative. Nonetheless, the one-sidedness of news reporting is striking. Hall also assumes that the Black young men charged with mugging had been 'fitted up' by the police or provoked into resisting arrest but of course there might have been actual crimes and real victims.

CONFLICT PERSPECTIVE: FEMINISM

Feminists complain that patterns and trends in crime are misleading because they don't represent the full extent of the violence and harassment directed towards women. They do not think that this crime has meaningfully declined in the last 20 years so the **Great Crime Decline** (p95) has not reduced the victimisation of women.

4th Wave Feminism points to 'unofficial' victim surveys like the **2012 Sexual Assault Survey** by *Mumsnet* (p86) and more recently **Soma Sara's Everyone's Invited** website (**2020**), both of which invite women and girls to report their testimonies of sexual abuse.

Research: go back over your notes on **Peer Groups** as agencies of social control for **1A: Socialisation, Culture & Identity** and remind yourself about **Everyone's Invited**.

The problem is that the only evidence for these patterns and trends comes from victim surveys, many of which are highly **unstructured** and **unreliable**. There's no doubt that female victimisation is higher than **official crime statistics** show, but how much higher is not clear.

RESEARCH PROFILE: BATES (2014)

Laura Bates launched the Everyday Sexism Project online in 2012. The website invites women to contribute their personal stories of daily sexism, from street harassment to workplace discrimination to sexual assault and rape.

Bates expected to gather 100 testimonies, but the Project has collected over 100,000 testimonies and launched new branches in 25 countries worldwide.

Bates wrote a book also titled *Everyday Sexism* (2014) to reflect on the meaning of these testimonies of being groped on public transport or verbally abused by passing strangers.

Laura Bates (photo: Conway Hall)

Bates argues this behaviour is **normalised**: we accept it as normal, even though we shouldn't, which explains why it is **rarely reported**: *"... every woman I spoke to had a story. And they weren't random one-off events, but reams of tiny pinpricks – like my own experiences – so niggling and normalised that to protest about each one felt trivial. Yet put them together, and the picture was strikingly clear."*

The idea of normalised sexually abusive behaviour is sometimes termed **'rape culture'** and it is an example of **social construction**: a criminal act that is not viewed as a crime.

Research: visit https://everydaysexism.com and reflect on some of the testimonies.

SOCIAL ACTION PERSPECTIVE: INTERACTIONISM

Interactionists view patterns and trends as part of the **social construction** of crime (p83). This means they tell us a lot about the attitudes and values of the people who define and measure crime, but not so much about what the public are doing.

For example, Labelling Theorists like **Howard Becker** regard 'criminal' as a social label that is applied to some people but not to others. If burglary has declined since 2003 (as trends suggest) then this doesn't necessarily mean that thieves have stopped breaking into people's houses; it just means victims no longer think it's worth involving the police (they contact their insurers instead) and the police no longer record such things as crimes.

On the other hand, if hate crimes have increased since 2016 (as trends suggest), it doesn't mean more bigots are attacking people that they discriminate against; it just means victims who used to regard themselves as having been assaulted or mugged are now considering themselves the victim of a hate crime and the police are increasingly recording it as such.

This means that the **Great Crime Decline** (p95) might really just be a decline in people reporting crimes and the police recording them.

This is an important insight into the social construction of crime and worth bearing in mind before you read too much into shocking figures about crime waves – but it tends to result in patterns and trends being dismissed as meaningless, which doesn't help with assessing crime prevention strategies or helping victims.

RESEARCH PROFILE: COHEN (1972)

Stan Cohen (1942–2013) wrote a classic in media studies, *Folk Devils & Moral Panics* (1972). Cohen researched the fights which took place in English seaside resorts on Bank Holidays in 1964 between two youth subcultures: the **Mods** and the **Rockers**. Cohen's study was a mixture of observation, content analysis (looking at the language and images of the 1964 news reports) and interviews. He concludes that the media reporting was very different from the actual events, but it had a huge influence on the subsequent behaviour of the youths and the police. In effect, the Media *creates* the deviance rather than just reporting it.

Cohen suggests that there are five groups involved in the process of moral panic. There is the **threat** that starts the moral panic, which Cohen calls a "**folk devil**." There are **enforcers of laws**, like the police. There is the **news media** reporting on it and attaching symbolic images to it. There are **politicians**, who sometimes add to the panic. Finally, there is **the public**, which becomes concerned about the threat and demands something be done about it.

This study supports the idea that news stories are **socially constructed** rather than **social facts** and that the reporting of crime influences the way statistics are compiled. However, it might not be representative of interactive and video-driven 21st century news.

PATTERNS & TRENDS: A TOOLKIT

You are expected to know about four main types of patterns/trends and could be asked to focus on either **offending** (who is committing crimes) or **victimisation** (who the victims are). Most research suggests that the average offender and the average victim are very similar: male, working class and aged 18-24. They are disproportionately likely to be Black.

SOCIAL DISTRIBUTION BY SOCIAL CLASS

We have already seen that **self-report studies** show that offending behaviour in working class and middle classes youths is very similar (p92). However, there is a perception that crime is a working class phenomenon, with the middle classes viewed as 'respectable' and 'law abiding.' Fear of crime is high among middle class households, who own expensive possessions and invest in security measures like burglar alarms. But do the figures bear this stereotype out?

Offending

According to **National Prison Survey (2020)**, 41% of male convicts come from unskilled or skilled manual classes. **Robert Reiner (2007)** claims that 74% of the prison population is drawn from the poorest 20% of the population.

According to the **Mayor of London's Office (2019)**, three-quarters of the boroughs in London with the highest levels of violent offending are also in the top 10 most deprived, while the same boroughs also have higher proportions of children living in poverty than the London average. This certainly links crime to deprivation and low social class.

The main criticism is that these patterns reflect who gets caught rather than who offends. Wealthy and educated offenders are more likely to carry out crimes that go undetected (e.g. **white collar crime**) and avoid conviction if caught because they can afford good lawyers.

Victimisation

The **CSEW** (p90) doesn't collect data on social class of victims but there are other measures. For example, in 2020, only 1.2% of homeowners were victims of violent crime but this rose to 2.5% for people privately renting, doubling the risk. Home ownership is associated with the wealthy middle class and poorer people are more likely to rent.

The two groups most at risk of violent crime are the unemployed and students (source: **ONS, 2020**). Since students are more likely to be middle class than working class, this suggests that a similar lifestyle is the main factor, such as being out late, traveling on foot/public transport rather than driving, living in poorer neighbourhoods and living in insecure accommodation.

Research: visit https://www.ons.gov.uk/visualisations/dvc432/content.html and input different background details into the **Risk of Crime Calculator**

AO2 ILLUSTRATION: THE SHANNON MATTHEWS CASE

In 2008, 10-year-old **Shannon Matthews** disappeared from her home in West Yorkshire, followed by appeals on national TV from her mother Karen. 24 days later Shannon was discovered by the police in a house belonging to a relative of Karen Matthew's boyfriend. It soon became clear that Karen Matthews had arranged her daughter's disappearance (and kept her sedated with a travel sickness drug) in order for the relative to claim the £50,000 reward for later finding her.

There was a lot of public outrage and much of it was directed at the chaotic family life that Shannon grew up in. The Matthews family, living on benefits and trying to make money out of their children, resembled the **Underclass** described by the **New Right** (p122) as well as the stereotype of immoral **Chavs** that was popular at the time.

Some commentators pointed out how the local working class community had united to search for missing Shannon, but this had received very little praise in the news media. The story illustrates working class families as both offenders *and* victims, but also the way in which the media stigmatises the working classes (i.e. presents them negatively).

RESEARCH PROFILE: JONES (2011)

Owen Jones is a Marxist journalist and activist whose book *Chavs* (2011) exposes negative stereotyping of the poor. 'Chavs' was a term popular in the early 2000s for anti-social youths from deprived backgrounds, wearing sportswear and (often counterfeit) brands like Burberry. Chav seems to come from a Romany word for 'youth' but it is (wrongly) interpreted as being a code for Council Housed And Violent.

Jones argues that middle class contempt for 'Chavs' is another example of **stigmatising** the working classes and a **moral panic** fuelled by the news media. The effect is to divide the working class against each other and justify excluding them from politics, public places and serious consideration.

Jones' argument resembles **Pearson**'s study of Hooligans (p85), **Cohen**'s earlier study of Mods and Rockers as folk devils in the 1960s (p101) and **Hall**'s study of the Black mugger as a scapegoat in the 1970s (p99). Jones has been criticised for treating the working class as homogeneous and not recognising their freewill. **Lynsey Hanley (2011)** points out that that *"a great deal of chav-bashing goes on within working-class neighbourhoods."*

SOCIAL DISTRIBUTION BY GENDER

The gender divide in crime is stark, with males overwhelmingly being the main offenders and also most likely to be victims. This is often linked to characteristics like aggression and risk-taking in males, due either to **biological factors** (like the male hormone testosterone) or **socialisation** (with females socialised to be more compliant). However, this divide can be questioned.

Offending

Official crime statistics consistently show males responsible for at least 80% of crimes. In 2019, males make up 85% of all arrests and women are more likely to appear in court for less severe offences, like driving offences which make up 55% of females but only 29% of males. The average male prison sentence is 19.7 months compared to 11.3 months for females. Males are responsible for 74% of violent crime (source: **ONS, 2019**).

The Youth Justice Board (2009) shows that the peak age for female offending is 15, but it is 18 for males. This suggests that females start deviant behaviour earlier (but perhaps with less serious transgressions) then grow out of it, whereas male deviance continues into their 20s with much more serious consequences.

However, female offending (so-called 'pink collar crime') seems to be rising. According to the **Institute for Criminal Policy Research (2017)**, in the 21st century the global female prison population increased by a half while males went up by a fifth.

This shift might be due to increasing gender equality in society and women experiencing many of the same economic pressures as men (e.g. being the breadwinner for the household) or technology like the Internet making crime more accessible to women.

The **Chivalry Thesis** (p104) offers another view: women are treated more leniently by police and the courts due to gender stereotyping and **police discretion**, so their offending does not get recorded to the same degree as men. To combat this, **Europol (2019)** invited 21 EU states to submit their 'most wanted' fugitive for a *'Crime Has No Gender'* campaign and 18 were female.

Research: visit Europol's *'Crime Has No Gender'* campaign at https://www.europol.europa.eu/newsroom/news/crime-has-no-gender-meet-europe%E2%80%99s-most-wanted-female-fugitives and study the 'most wanted' offenders

Victimisation

Males make up 3.9% of victims of crime, compared to females 3.4%. 64% of homicide victims are male, compared to 36% being female. Men are twice as likely to be victims of violent crime (experienced by 2.3% compared to 1.2% of women). However, when it comes to crimes like domestic abuse, victimisation rises to 7.3% for females and 3.6% for males, doubling the female risk (source: **ONS, 2019**).

Moreover, the **Islington Crime Survey** (p90) revealed in stark terms the 'curfew on women' imposed by the fear of crime and sexual assault after dark. The campaigning organisation **Femicide (2018)** carried out a census showing 1428 women were killed by men over 10 years, which is one killing every three days. 4.9 million women report sexual assault in their lives and 1.4 million have faced rape; the figures for men are a fifth of that, while 98.5% of rapists are male (source: **ONS, 2021**).

AO2 ILLUSTRATION: THE MURDER OF SARAH EVERARD

In 2021, 33-year-old **Sarah Everard** was abducted and murdered when walking home at night past Clapham Common in London. The murderer turned out to be a serving Metropolitan police officer. The case prompted outrage regarding the violence directed at women by men and the dangers for women in traveling freely. A vigil held for Sarah Everard was attended by many Feminist groups but there was controversy when it was forcefully dispersed by the police (due to restrictions on assembling during the 2020-22 Coronavirus Pandemic).

A later protest was called the **97 March** after a survey for **UN Women (2021)** revealed that 97% of women have been sexually harassed. **Baroness Jenny Jones** made the suggestion that there should be a **'curfew on men'** which would *make women a lot safer.*" Jones' argument was that instead of expecting women to restrict themselves to be safe (not leaving home after dark, not traveling alone), we should expect men to experience these inconveniences since they are the perpetrators. The fact that women are blamed if they fail to protect themselves reveals the **social construction** of crime (p83).

RESEARCH PROFILE: ADLER (1975)

Freda Adler is a Feminist who wrote *Sisters In Crime* **(1975)**. She examines data from the 1960s to show a growing trend for female criminality and she predicts that this trend will accelerate. Adler proposes a **Liberation Thesis** that growing freedom for women enables them to leave the domestic sphere (the home) and find work. This causes them to develop traditionally masculine traits like aggression and risk-taking and exposes them to opportunities for committing crime that never used to be available.

Adler's argument resembles a **Functionalist** one – that crime is regrettable, but it is a necessary side-effect of something good, which is progress. She is supported by **Carolyn Jackson (2006)** who reports a growing culture of 'Laddish' behaviour in schoolgirls.

However, Adler's original data set was too small to draw confident conclusions from and female crime has not accelerated as she predicted. **Estrada et al. (2015)** suggests that women are not becoming more like men but rather the other way around: the offending rate for men is dropping, closing the gender gap with women.

SOCIAL DISTRIBUTION BY ETHNICITY

In the **2011 Census**, 83% of the UK population identify as White, 8% Asian and 3% Black. You would expect this distribution to appear in crime figures too, with 83% of offences carried out by White people and 83% of the victims of crime being White. The fact that this distribution does *not* appear is troubling for sociologists.

Offending

The arrest rate for the White population is 10 arrests per 1,000 people; this rises to 18 for Mixed Race and 32 for Black. This is a startling difference in arrests. The rate for the Asian population in the UK is 12 (only 6 for Indian) and the lowest rate is 3 per 1,000 people for Chinese. 21% of those convicted of homicide are Black compared to 67% White (source: **ONS, 2019**).

Similarly, 73% of the UK prison population identity as White and 27% as Black, Asian or other minority ethnic groups (source: **Ministry of Justice, 2019**).

One explanation for this is that these populations commit more crime. This is the explanation preferred by **Functionalists** who treat such data as **social facts**. In support of this, ethnicity tends to intersect with **social class**, with Black populations in the UK being more likely to be poor and Indian and Chinese more likely to be wealthy.

However, another explanation is **institutional (or systemic) racism** in the criminal justice system (CJD). The police might be more likely to stop and search Black youths, more like to arrest them if they see something suspicious and courts might be more likely to convict them of offences. **Geoff Pearson & Mike Rowe (2020)** spent 7 years observing UK police officers carrying out stop & search and conclude its use with Black suspects is disproportionate. **Holdaway**'s research (p88) found a racist occupational culture in the Metropolitan police in the 1970s.

Hall's study of racist moral panics in the news (p99) points out that there are pressures from the news media to target Black suspects.

However, the argument for racist bias in the CJD struggles to account for the low rate of offending in Indian or Chinese ethnic groups.

Victimisation

Most ethnic groups have broadly similar levels of victimisation (13% on average) but the Mixed Ethnicity group stands out for the high rate of victimisation: 21% for males and 19% for females (source: **ONS, 2020**).

However, Black people in the UK have a higher risk of being victims of homicide, 5.6 times higher than White people throughout the 21st century and increasing since 2015. This experience **intersects with age**, with Black youths aged 16-24 being 10.6 times more likely to be victims of homicide: 49% of Black victims, compared to 25% Asian or 12% White (source: **ONS, 2019**).

There is a tendency for crime to be **intra-racial**. This means offenders are more likely to commit crimes against people of the *same* racial group as themselves. This might explain the high victimisation for Mixed Race individuals, if they belong to more than one group.

AO2 ILLUSTRATION: THE MURDER OF STEPHEN LAWRENCE

Stephen Lawrence was 18 years old when he was killed in 1993 in a racist attack. He had been waiting for a bus with a friend, when a gang of White racists attacked them both. Stephen's friend escaped and called the police, but Stephen died from his injuries.

The Metropolitan Police's investigation was flawed from the start. For example, their initial suspect was Stephen's friend. They did not pursue the gang, although they were already known racists. When the suspects were brought to trial, the case collapsed because of weak evidence collected by the police.

Eventually, in 2012, two of Stephen's killers were convicted when new evidence emerged. Before that, in 1999, the **Macpherson Report** (p129) into the case concluded that the Metropolitan Police were *"institutionally racist"* (echoing accusation made by **Holdaway** in the 1970s, p88). Dr Neville Lawrence said that his son's murder *"opened the country's eyes"* to racism.

The case of Stephen Lawrence suggests that the way crimes against Black people are investigated makes it hard to know whether the **social distribution of crime by ethnicity** is reliably measured.

Research: find out more about Stephen Lawrence, the police investigation and its outcomes

RESEARCH PROFILE: FITZGERALD ET AL. (2002)

Marion Fitzgerald and colleagues conducted the **Policing for London Survey** in the aftermath of the **Stephen Lawrence** case. They interviewed people stopped by the Metropolitan Police and found many were satisfied with their treatment but measured a decline in confidence in the police during the 1980s and 1990s. Dissatisfaction with the police was highest among three groups: young people, Black people and people living in deprived areas. The best predictors of being stopped by the police were *"being young, being male, being black, being working class and being single"* – which indicates how patterns in crime are affected by **Intersectionality**.

This supports the contention that policing practices are **institutionally racist**. It only describes the Metropolitan Police of 20 years ago and doesn't account for reforms since then, such as the Metropolitan Police recruiting Black and minority ethnic officers.

SOCIAL DISTRIBUTION BY AGE

In 1901, the UK population had a high proportion of children (32% aged under 15) and a small elderly population (only 5% aged 65+). In 2018, the proportions of people in these two age groups were the same (18% for each). This shows the UK has an ageing population: people are living longer and having fewer children (source: **ONS, 2020**).

As society has more and more elderly people in it and proportionally fewer young people, you would expect this to affect patterns and trends of crime, with less crime by the young but more elderly victims of crime. However, these patterns aren't obvious.

Offending

Stereotypes have always presented adolescents and young adults as impulsive and rule-breaking, compared to more retrained and law-abiding older people. Crime increases in early adolescence (age 14), peaks in the 20s, and then declines. This statistical shape has been termed the **age–crime curve** (**Roque et al, 2015**).

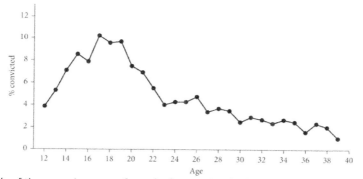

*An example of the age-crime curve from the famous Cambridge Study (**Farrington et al, 1995**)*

Declining proportions of young people in society might explain the **Great Crime Decline** (p95). However, prison populations tell a different story, with 30-39 year olds making up 32% of UK prisoners, with much smaller numbers of younger and older convicts.

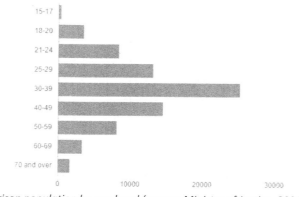

Prison population by age band (source: Ministry of Justice, 2021)

This is probably because more serious crimes (and a history of previous offending) make it more likely a person will get a custodial (prison) sentence; also, prisoners on long sentences might have entered prison when they were much younger. According to the **Joseph Rowntree Foundation (JRF)** only about 5% of males are **chronic offenders** who persist in criminal behaviour, going on to become long-term prisoners, but the majority of young people abandon crime as they get older.

Victimisation

Young people are certainly at risk of victimisation: those aged 20-29 made up 13% of the UK population but are the victims in 27% of violent crimes; people aged 80+ make up 5% of the population but are victims in less than 1% of violent crimes (source: **ONS, 2021**). As with **social class** (p101), this is certainly linked to lifestyle, with older people more likely to stay at home in secure accommodation and avoid traveling on foot, at night or interacting often with strangers.

Young women aged 20-24 are more likely to be victims of domestic abuse (15.1% of cases) than older women – and women aged 16-19 are the next most victimised group for this (source: **ONS, 2019**).

Older people are more likely to be victims of crimes like fraud, with 12% of people aged 65+ reporting being victims of fraud in a year; the elderly make up 8 out of every 10 victims of doorstep scams (source: **ONS, 2019**).

There is little evidence to support the idea that older people have more **fear of crime**, but they do perceive themselves to be more **vulnerable** to crime and take more precautions against it, which perhaps explains why they are less likely to be victims (source: **Köber et al, 2020**).

Zombie knives (photo: Flossy Carter)

AO2 ILLUSTRATION: KNIFE CRIME

In 2020, there were 46,000 knife crimes, 51% higher than in 2011 when the government started keeping track of knife crimes specifically – and that figure excludes Greater Manchester Police which could not provide data. According to the CSEW, knives account for 9% of all violent crime and 1 in 5 such attackers are under 18. The majority of the attacks are in London (source: **ONS, 2020**).

Various factors are blamed for the 'epidemic' of knife crime in UK cities: disputes between drug-dealing gangs, social media glorifying violence, the closure of youth clubs and mental health issues brought on by lockdowns during the 2020-22 Coronavirus Pandemic. Others blame the declining use of Stop & Search by the police. In 2016, the sale of **'Zombie Knives'** was banned: these giant blades with serrated edges are collected by horror fans but were used in attacks.

Research: find out more about the increase in knife crimes and plans to deal with it

RESEARCH PROFILE: FARRINGTON ET AL. (2006)

David Farrington conducted the famous **Cambridge Study** which is a massive longitudinal study of 411 boys from the East End of London who were born in 1953-4. The study began when the boys were 8-9. It involved interviews with the boys, their parents and teachers as well as gathering medical data, school reports and police reports.

There were follow-up **self-report** interviews as the cohort aged. By age 48, 93% were still alive and interviewed. Of this group of 404, 360 had criminal records. Their offending had peaked at age 17. A small number (7%) were defined as **chronic offenders** because they accounted for half of the offences recorded by the study: on average, their criminal careers lasted from age 14-35.

The proportion leading successful (non-criminal) lives was 78% at age 32 but rose to 88% at 48 – the reformed offenders were no different in life success from the ones with no convictions.

There are lots of dates for the Cambridge Study, which is updated regularly, but big reports came out in 1982, 1995 and this data is from 2006.

Farrington concludes that the factors involved in criminality are family histories of crime, poverty, impulsive personality traits, poor parenting and poor school performance. He recommends targeting at-risk children to reduce future offending.

Farrington's study only considers males from a White working class background. Despite this, Farrington's results closely resemble national patterns today in the life course of offenders. Another longitudinal self-report study, the **Edinburgh Study of Youth Transitions and Crime (ESYTC)**, has a cohort of 4300 young people who started secondary school in 1998. This study focuses on gender difference and has a cohort from 'this side' of the **Great Crime Decline** (p95), but they are still too old to have grown up through the knife crime epidemic.

GLOBAL PATTERNS: ORGANISED CRIME

Globalisation is explored in **Section A**. It challenges ideas about crime because crime is normally defined as breaking a country's laws, but global crime goes beyond any one country. There are some international crime agencies that seek out and punish such criminals (e.g. **Interpol**) but global crime is also tackled by military intervention; e.g. after the 911 bombings, the USA and allies invaded Afghanistan, where the terrorist organisers were based.

As well as terrorism, global organised crime is involved in drug smuggling, people trafficking, arms dealing, cyber crime and identity theft, kidnapping, counterfeiting and extortion (threatening people to get money). It includes people smugglers sending migrants across the sea in dinghies, scammers emailing you from Nigeria and pirates capturing ships off the coast of Somalia. It also includes famous crime cartels like the **Mafia**. The **Global Financial Integrity Report (2017)** states that *"transnational crime is a business, and business is very good"* and estimates that global crime makes between $1.6-2.2 *trillion* a year.

A trillion is a thousand billion. If you stacked a trillion dollars, the pile would stretch all the way to the sun. With a trillion dollars, you could buy the oil company Exxon Mobil and have enough left to buy McDonald's and Coca-Cola too.

Hobbs & Dunningham (1998) studied how organised crime has expanded from large but national crime organisations to transnational crime organisations on the back of globalisation. They suggest that this has led to the decline of tightly organised groups like the Mafia. Instead, global crime operates through a **'glocal'** system –a global network built from local connections. For example, local opium-growers deliver their product to a drug cartel with an international supply chain (with enough wealth and power to get the product over national borders) which then sells heroin on to local dealers at the other end.

AO2 ILLUSTRATION: THE MAFIA

The term 'Mafia' is used for any organised crime group, but the word comes from Sicily and was used to describe the ***Cosa Nostra***, a Sicilian crime subculture. The **American Mafia** became powerful and wealthy smuggling alcohol during 1920s Prohibition; it was linked to Italian-American families and included the famous gangster **Al Capone**. These Mafia groups were often based around family ties, with a boss (***don***), his lieutenants (***capos***) and their soldiers. The groups maintained a code of ***omerta*** (secrecy). However, in the 1980s and '90s a number of high profile cases in Italy and the USA convicted powerful Mafia leaders by getting gangsters to break the *omerta* code and testify against each other.

Since then, new Mafia organisations have appeared, notably in the former-USSR, such as the **Russian Mafia** and **Bulgarian Mafia**. However, these groups operate more like businesses than families and don't have the rituals, honour-code or link to a supportive community base.

Research: find out more about the Mafia; watch the classic films *The Godfather* (1972) or *Goodfellas* (1990); research other organised crime groups like the Chinese Triads, Japanese Yakuza, South American drug cartels and the Golden Triangle

RESEARCH PROFILE: GLENNY (2008)

Misha Glenny wrote the book *McMafia* **(2008)**, examining the way organised crime adapts to Globalisation. The title links to **Ritzer**'s concept of **'McDonaldisation'** in society (*c.f.* **Section A**, p51) and suggests that organised crime has transformed in the same way. The book inspired a 2018 TV drama series.

Glenny suggests that organised criminal gangs have become very influential in areas of the world where there is **weak rule of law** (e.g. failed states such as Afghanistan), widespread **distrust of the state** (e.g. Mexico), a landscape that makes areas **inaccessible** (e.g. Colombia with its rainforest) and high levels of **corruption**.

Glenny argues that a significant criminal network operates from **Bulgaria**, which is a 'hub' connecting the rich and poor parts of the world. The Mafia have held considerable power there since the collapse of Communism in 1989. Glenny links the Bulgarian Mafia to most of the drugs and prostitutes that are bought in the UK.

"A smart, outraged, and vividly described whirlwind tour of criminal conspiracy.... Clear, compelling, and scary."
—*The Christian Science Monitor*

MISHA GLENNY

McMAFIA

A JOURNEY THROUGH THE GLOBAL CRIMINAL UNDERWORLD

With a New Foreword

Glenny explores other networks, such as gunrunners in Ukraine, money launderers in Dubai, drug syndicates in Canada and cyber criminals in Brazil. Glenny takes a **Marxist** approach that this crime is generated by Capitalism itself. He argues that, since drugs account for 70% of the profits of global crime, legalising drugs would be the best way of reducing the power of these criminals. However, he underestimates the importance of **glocalisation** because he makes organisations like the Mafia so important to his analysis.

GLOBAL PATTERNS: GREEN CRIME

Green crime – or environmental crime – is also linked to **Globalisation** as environmental damage caused in one country can affect its neighbours or even the entire planet. It includes illegal pollution and dumping toxic waste but also **poaching** and the destruction of endangered species. Poaching is part of a multimillion-dollar industry that is part of **organised global crime**. However, a lot of environmental damage is caused by legitimate businesses 'cutting corners' and ignoring regulations that are supposed to protect the environment for the sake of profit.

'Green crime' is a term coined by **Michael J Lynch (1990)** and it is an example of **transgressive criminology**. This means that many of the 'crimes' studied here are not literally crimes – or else they occupy loop-holes or grey areas in international law – but transgressive criminologists argue that since they cause harm on a global scale, they are transgressions (wrong-doing) that should be *treated* as crimes. These criminologists are also activists, trying to change laws to make such things literally illegal instead of just transgressive.

Rob White (2008) divides green crime into two types of harm.

- **Anthropocentric Harm:** harm to the environment from the perspective of humanity; e.g. pollution damages the water supply or causes diseases that then harms humans.
- **Ecocentric Harm:** sees harm to any aspect of the environment as transgressive whether it impacts humans or not; e.g. animal cruelty or the destruction of habitats, regardless of whether there is any specific human cost.

Nigel South (2008) talks about two other types of green crime:

- **Primary Green Crime:** is committed directly against the environment or causes harm to the environment; e.g. pollution, deforestation, animal cruelty
- **Secondary Green Crime:** undermines the rules regarding protecting the environment, e.g: violence against environmental groups, bribery/corruption to get round regulations

Transgressive criminology is difficult to put into practice. By focusing on 'harm' rather than laws, the idea of Green Crime becomes very **subjective**; almost anything can be Green Crime. For example, should *all* meat production or even consumption of meat be a Green Crime, or just meat farmed with cruel methods?

Nonetheless, the idea of transgressive criminology is popular with **Conflict** sociologists who regard the actual laws as the creations of privileged groups (**Marxists** point to wealthy Capitalists, **Feminists** point to men) and see the job of a sociologists to question the **social construction** (p83) of law. **Consensus** sociologists see laws as the expression of our culture and are inclined to view Green Crime as a crime if it breaks laws, but not as any sort of crime at all if it doesn't.

Rainbow Warrior (photo: Hans van Dijk)

AO2 ILLUSTRATION: GREENPEACE & *RAINBOW WARRIOR*

Greenpeace is a non-governmental campaigning group founded in 1971 and based out of the Netherlands but with offices in 55 countries. It campaigns for the protection of the environment and the exposing and prevention of Green Crime. Its aim is to *"ensure the ability of the Earth to nurture life in all its diversity."* It opposes climate change, deforestation, overfishing, whaling, genetic engineering and nuclear power.

You will notice that not all of Greenpeace's targets fit the ordinary definition of a crime and some (like nuclear power) are presented by other groups as **solutions** *to environmental problems – this shows transgressive criminology in action but also the problem with it.*

Greenpeace uses boats to protest over-fishing, commercial whaling and nuclear testing at sea and *Rainbow Warrior* was the flagship. In 1985, *Rainbow Warrior* sailed to New Zealand to protest French nuclear testing in the Pacific. The French Intelligence Service (DGSE) planted bombs on the ship and sank it. A photographer on board was killed, two French spies were arrested, and France paid Greenpeace $8.1 million in compensation.

The sinking of *Rainbow Warrior* is an example of a **secondary green crime**.

RESEARCH PROFILE: BECK (1992)

Ulrich Beck published *The Risk Society* **(1992)** in response to the 1988 nuclear disaster at **Chernobyl**, in which a nuclear reactor leaked radioactive pollution across Europe. Beck explains Green Crime as part **'the risk society,'** arguing that industrial societies create new risks because of modern technologies that were unknown in the past. Because we have no previous experiences of risks of this sort, we are not well equipped to weigh them up or manage them.

Do Beck's ideas sound familiar? They are echoed by **Giddens'** *concept of* **manufactured risk** *(p10) that was introduced in* **Section A**.

Beck claims that one new 'risky technology' is nuclear power, which generates small quantities of highly toxic waste which stays radioactive for thousands of years. Beck argues that environmental problems are global – he states that *"smog is democratic"* meaning that pollution affects everyone equally regardless of your background.

Beck doesn't offer any solutions to the problem of Green Crime; he just points out that this is a new problem that cannot be tackled using traditional ideas and policies. This means he supports **transgressive criminology** rather than the view that environmental crime is just another type of global crime – or not really a crime at all.

Beck isn't strictly a **Postmodernist** *– like Giddens, he believes we are in* **Late Modernity** *– but his ideas about risk resemble a Postmodern diagnosis of contemporary problems.*

AO2 ILLUSTRATION: THE 2011 LONDON RIOTS

In the summer of 2011, there was a week of rioting in towns and cities across England, but largely in London and starting in Tottenham. TV viewers were shocked to see battles with the police, the burning of cars, buses and shops as well as looting on a huge scale. There were 5 deaths and over £200 million in property damage.

The police made over 3000 arrests and courts had to open for extended hours to process all the cases. An instruction came from the Conservative Government that rioters be punished with strong sentences, including 4 years for a man who stayed home but encouraged rioting via *Facebook*.

While 12% of the working-age population of the UK are on benefits of some sort, 35% of the adults prosecuted after the riots were on benefits. Some commentators took this as evidence for the link between class and crime – or for the **New Right**'s idea of the crime-prone **Underclass** (p121).

While 49% of the population of the UK in 2011 were male, 90% of the adults prosecuted after the riots were male. This could be evidence for the link between males and crime.

While 3% of the population of the UK in 2011 was Black – rising to 11% in London as a whole – 50% of the adults prosecuted after the riots were Black. Some commentators took this as evidence for the link between ethnicity and crime – or for the **Neo-Marxist** idea of the police targeting Black working class people disproportionately through **selective policing** (p92).

London riots (photo: StuartBannock)

EXAM PRACTICE: PATTERNS & TRENDS IN CRIME

The OCR exam has three questions in **Paper 3 Section B**. Questions 7-9 are on Education and questions 10-12 are on Religion, Belief & Faith, but this Study Guide is focused on **Option 1** which covers questions **4-6**:

4. In what ways is victimisation distributed by gender? **[10 marks: 6 AO1 + 4 AO2]**

This is one of those 'describe & illustrate' questions, but with no Source A or Source B to lean on. No need to evaluate.

Make two sociological points about victimisation – perhaps a point about males and a point about females. It's a good idea to refer to particular statistics (like 64% of homicide victims being male) and you should definitely use some sociological terminology (like the Dark Figure or the Great Crime Decline). Then offer examples of victimisation and make sure each example has an explanation linked to gender. For example, "Males are more at risk from homicide and this might be because they are also more likely to commit homicide."

5. To what extent is green crime a growing problem? **[20 marks: 8 AO1 + 4 AO2 + 8 AO3]**

This is a mid-size essay with a requirement for developed evaluation. You should spend 25 minutes and write at least 500 words.

*Write **three** points. Each point should introduce a sociological idea with some illustration from the real world. Each point should finish off with a developed evaluation (see **Chapter 9** for this). For example, you could write about ecocentric crimes, secondary green crimes and transgressive criminology. Make sure you mention **Beck**'s study on risk and be sure to answer the question: are green crimes growing or not?*

6. Outline and evaluate the view that ethnicity is important for understanding patterns and trends in crime. **[40 marks: 16 AO1 + 8 AO2 + 16 AO3]**

This is the last of the two big (40 mark) essays in OCR A-Level Sociology. You should spend 50 minutes and write at least 1000 words.

*Write **four** points. Each point should introduce a sociological idea with some illustration from the real world. Each point should finish off with a developed evaluation (see **Chapter 9** for this). For example, you could write about the ethnic groups as offenders, then as victims, then the Dark Figure of unrecorded crime, police institutional racism and finish with either **Fitzgerald et al.** or **Holdaway** criticising the Metropolitan Police. Be sure to come to a conclusion: is ethnicity important or is class, age or gender more significant?*

CHAPTER 7 – EXPLAINING CRIME & DEVIANCE

Crime and deviance can be explained by a number of *"theoretical views"* that match the Perspectives you have learned about earlier in the course. However, a few new criminology Perspectives are introduced as well: **Realism (Left** & **Right)** and **Subcultural Theories**.

Positive Views of Crime & Deviance

It might seem strange to have a 'positive' view of crime, especially if you've been a victim of it. However, crime has its up-sides and not just for the criminals.

Crime stimulates the economy because stolen or vandalised goods have to be replaced, often with superior one. This means a demand for manufacturing, trade in the shops and income for insurance companies. People also buy security equipment (locks, alarms, CCTV).

Crime reinforces communities, which band together in adversity. Neighbourhood Watch schemes encourage people to keep an eye on each other's property and entire communities come together during crises (like the townsfolk searching for the missing **Shannon Matthews**, p102). When people discuss crime and express their outrage and pity, they reinforce society's norms and values.

Crime can act as a way for people to 'vent' frustrations and express unhappiness. This argument is often used with respect to prostitution, asserting (often without evidence) that if men did not visit prostitutes, they would commit rape. A less controversial example is rioting, which expresses dissatisfaction with the police and/or the government and can be a trigger for social reform.

This viewpoint is associated with **Functionalism** (p119) but **Neo-Marxists** argue that crime is important resistance to Capitalism (p126) and **4th Wave Feminists** sometimes argue that sex work is empowering for women (p130 and see the ideas of **Adler**, p105).

Negative Views of Crime & Deviance

A more common view is that crime is a bad thing, a cause of misery and fear, and it needs to be prevented wherever possible.

An important point made by **Left Realists** (p128) is that the rich have the wherewithal to replace stolen property and make themselves secure. Poor people, on the other hand, carry on suffering from the effects of crime even after the crime is over: lost goods, damaged self-esteem, insecurity, lost income while recovering. This is termed **multiple victimisation**, since the poor are hurt by crime in many more ways than the rich.

A similar point is made by **Feminists**, that crime is part of a culture of violent intimidation that oppresses women, restricts their movement and makes them dependent on men for protection (an uncertain protection, since male partners are the main source of domestic and sexual violence for women).

Even **Functionalists** have limits to the amount of crime they will tolerate as 'healthy' and they acknowledge that when crime becomes excessive, society becomes **dysfunctional**. The idea that society has already reached (or surpassed) this point of dysfunction is key to understanding the **New Right** Perspective (p122).

AO2 ILLUSTRATION: THE AMERICAN OPIOID EPIDEMIC

A crime problem that illustrates these views is the addiction to opioids in America. **Opioids** are pain-killing drugs that were heavily prescribed in the 1990s; they are strong, cheap but very addictive and an overdose can kill. Because they produce feelings of euphoria, they are popular as recreational drugs. They are supposed to be prescribed only to manage acute (temporary) pain, but America's private healthcare system combined with a black market means people can easily get long-term prescriptions or buy opioids illegally, often moving on to more dangerous opioids like heroin and fentanyl.

In 2020, nearly 70,000 Americans died from overdoses (more than die from motor accidents or shootings). Celebrities like the musicians Prince and Tom Petty and the actor Heath Ledger have died from overdoses involving opioids.

The opioid epidemic is certainly making profits for the makers of prescription painkillers and addiction is perhaps preferable to people rioting or carrying out rape or murder. However, the scale of the problem is a drag on the economy, since addicts aren't able to work or care for families and the USA has experienced a drop in life expectancy as a result, so Functionalists recognise it is **dysfunctional**. From a **Marxist** perspective, this is Big Pharma (the Capitalist medical industry) killing people to make money.

Research: find out more about the Opioid Epidemic, Big Pharma and the global trade in heroin and fentanyl

Opioid Epidemic (image by DES Daughter)

PERSPECTIVES ON CRIME & DEVIANCE

Perspectives are very broad viewpoints. They match the *"theoretical views"* the OCR Exam Board will assess you on. They are also important for evaluating **definitions and measures of crime and deviance** (p77) as well as how **patterns and trends** are interpreted (p97).

CONSENSUS PERSPECTIVE: FUNCTIONALISM

Functionalists usually take a **positive view** of crime and deviance. They regard crime as inevitable in all societies, partly because they acknowledge the role of human biology in shaping culture (and we are biologically evolved to be competitive and aggressive) and partly because, as **Durkheim's 'society of saints'** illustrates (p83), even highly moral communities will need to set boundaries on what is acceptable and therefore create the possibility of deviance. Durkheim adds that *"crime brings together upright consciences"* – by sharing our outrage at crime and pity for its victims, we reaffirm our culture's norms and values.

Crime is also important for **boundary maintenance**. People need to know what the boundaries of acceptable behaviour are and what will happen if they cross them. Therefore, it is important that, every now and again, someone transgresses by crossing a boundary and the rest of the community see what the consequences are. That way, they are reassured that the boundaries matter. Otherwise, the importance of boundaries fades and people experience **anomie**, which is a state of meaninglessness and detachment from society. Anomie can drive people to suicide and drug-abuse (such as the **American Opioid Epidemic**, p118) and also to rioting and violence.

Functionalism is a **structuralist** Perspective, so the (bad) impact of crime on individuals is not as important as its overall impact on society, which is often good. This is like the old proverb, 'In order to make an omelette, you have to break a few eggs.' Many people find this view rather callous and as society becomes more **individualistic** (perhaps due to **Postmodernity**, *c.f.* **Section A**, p23) it becomes a less convincing position for many people.

For Functionalists, individuals only behave well if they are **socialised** by a supportive family and community. If people feel detached from society, they have no motivation to behave well. People also weigh up their decisions rationally, taking into account **risks and rewards**. Therefore, people will commit crime if they feel they can get away with it, if the punishments are not unpleasant or if they feel unobserved or that nobody will judge them badly.

This means that Functionalist views on **preventing crime** (p137) focus on tough policing, strict punishments and creating communities where people are observed by their neighbours. They particularly like the idea of communities policing themselves (e.g. electing their own sheriffs in the USA or local police commissioners in the UK).

RESEARCH PROFILE: MERTON (1938)

Robert K Merton (1910-2003) was an American **Functionalist** who explained the rising crime in Chicago in the 1930s by using Durkheim's idea of **anomie** to create **Strain Theory**.

Merton suggests that every society has **cultural goals** that people are **socialised** into striving for. There are **institutionalised means** of reaching those goals. In the USA, this is the 'American Dream' of getting qualifications and working hard to become successful and independent (a form of **meritocracy**). **Strain** occurs when not everybody has the resources needed to reach this goal (e.g. poor education, no job opportunities). People adapt to this strain in five ways:

Conformity: persevere with the institutionalised means to reach the cultural goals (e.g. study harder, work more hours)

Innovation: use unconventional means to reach the cultural goals (e.g. become a drug dealer or rob a bank)

Ritualism: persevere with the institutionalised means but abandon the cultural goals (e.g. plug away at a dead-end job or choose more modest goals for yourself)

Retreatism: abandon the institutionalised means *and* the cultural goals (e.g. drop out, become a homeless person or a drug addict or just live on benefits watching TV all day)

Rebellion: work to replace the institutionalised means and cultural goals with new ones (e.g. become a political activist, a religious radical or a terrorist)

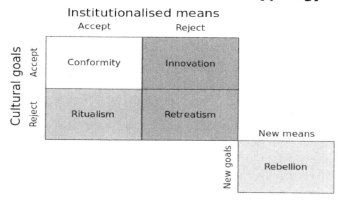

Robert K. Merton's Deviance Typology

Merton uses **official statistics** (p87) to develop Strain Theory and assumes that working class people commit crime to overcome the barriers placed in their way by an unfair society. However, he ignores **white collar crime** (why would already-successful people not conform?) and doesn't explain why most working class people remain law-abiding. His theory doesn't really explain violent crime or vandalism (**non-utilitarian crimes** that don't make you any richer).

Marxists would suggest that many criminals **internalise** the cultural goals, believing that they are only worthy of respect if they get rich (e.g. **Jock Young**'s concept of **social bulimia**, p125).

Subcultural Theories

Merton (like most Functionalists) assumes there is a **value consensus** about how to live which people only break with due to **anomie**. However, **Subcultural Theories** suggest that there might be **subcultures** in society with different value systems. Joining a **Criminal Subculture** and accepting its antisocial values would predispose you to committing crime.

Albert Cohen (1955, not the same Cohen who studied moral panics) suggests that working class boys experience **status frustration** when they cannot 'keep up' with middle class peers. They respond by joining an **Anti-School Subculture** where the values are inverted (flipped): it is bad to work hard and be praised by teachers, but good to cause trouble in class and get punished. Later, this subculture leads them into criminal behaviour too.

Cohen doesn't explain why most working-class boys carry on working hard at school. His theory doesn't explain girls and only covers **delinquency** in the teenage years, not adult criminality.

The biggest problem with Subcultural Theories is that they abandon a central premise of Functionalism: that there is value consensus in society. Merton suggests that criminals still have the same *goals* as law-abiding people, just different *means* of reaching them. But Cohen seems to suggest that anti-school working-class boys become something wholly 'other': lifelong deviants who view society from a completely topsy-turvy moral basis. This is closer to **Conflict Theory**, which argues that the interests and goals of the working class are completely at odds with the ruling class and only the brainwashing power of **ideology** makes them think the same.

RESEARCH PROFILE: CLOWARD & OHLIN (1960)

Cloward & Ohlin argue that, alongside the **legitimate opportunity structure** (school, jobs, careers – the **meritocracy**), there is an **illegitimate opportunity structure** (a career in crime). Just as not all people can access the legitimate opportunity structure (because of poor qualifications, unemployment, etc.), the illegitimate opportunity structures aren't available to everyone either.

Cloward & Ohlin identify three illegitimate opportunity structures: **(1) Criminal**, which is organised, like the **Mafia** (p110), with a 'career path' for young recruits that mirrors the legitimate meritocratic structures (bonuses for good work, promotions, etc.); **(2) Conflict**, where gangs compete over territory ("turf wars"), which is violent and only occasionally lucrative (some money from drugs or theft); **(3) Retreatist**, where groups who cannot join organised crime or gangs simply 'drop out' and become drug addicts.

Hobbs & Dunningham (1998, p111) criticise the idea that the Mafia are still dominant in **global organised crime**. Instead, there is a **'glocal'** network where the boundary between organised criminals and gangs blur. Cloward & Ohlin don't explore *why* working class males are denied access to legitimate opportunities or why only a minority of working class males actually join these illegitimate opportunity structures instead. They don't explain why women, who are also denied opportunities, aren't more involved in crime.

The New Right

The New Right could be considered a 'spin-off' from Functionalism in the 1980s. Its central assumption is that the vital **value consensus** has collapsed so emergency measures are needed to restore it. The New Right diagnoses the core institution for value consensus as the **nuclear family** (married parents and their children) and the biggest threat to this as the **Welfare State**. The Welfare State is the political arrangement that pays benefits to the poor and the unemployed.

Critics of the Welfare State argue it **rewards worklessness** and **undermines the family** (since couples are not forced to stay together for monetary reasons if the state pays for their children). The single parent family (especially the single mother with children) is a target for the New Right, who argue that single parents cannot effectively **socialise** their children, who grow up 'feral': the girls get pregnant without marrying and live on child benefits, repeating the cycle, while the boys search for a father-figure and join gangs.

The New Right identifies a **'benefits trap'** that means unemployed people would end up worse off if they took a job, creating an incentive to stay unemployed and leading to **generational unemployment**, where families have parents and grandparents who do not work and claim benefits. The solution is to cut back benefits, forcing healthy adults to find work and take responsibility for their families.

*These are controversial arguments. Many people (including, but not limited to, **Marxists**) would argue that unemployed people desperately want to work and the stereotype of a chaotic and immoral families on benefits is a news media stereotype (see the case of **Shannon Matthews**, p102).*

Research: revisit your notes on **1A; Socialisation, Culture & Identity** and link these ideas to **social control in the workforce** – including the arguments by the **Joseph Rowntree Foundation (2012)** and **Macmillan (2011)** that cast doubt on the existence of the Underclass.

The New Right could be seen as a variation of **Subcultural Theory**, proposing just a single subculture, the Underclass, as responsible for society's problems. It 'others' the Underclass, demonising them as feral and antisocial, and this breaks away from the Functionalist idea of value consensus.

The New Right is condemned by **Marxists**, especially **Left Realists** (p128), for blaming crime on the very people who are most likely to be victims of it. Marxists object to the idea that poor people choose to live in poverty and lack a basic sense of right and wrong. **Jock Young (2003)** calls it a *"sociology of vindictiveness"* that tries to *"punish, demean and humiliate"* the poor.

Feminists criticise the New Right for demonising single mothers. Many Feminists regard it as an achievement to be celebrated that women can get away from abusive male partners and they do not support policies that would force unhappy couples to stay together or make mothers financially dependent on a man's earnings.

RESEARCH PROFILE: MURRAY (1984, 1989, 1999)

Charles Murray wrote the influential book *Losing Ground* (1984) which is the key statement of New Right thinking. Murray traces the rise of crime in the USA since the 1960s and finds it does not match trends in unemployment; however, it does match the trend for children born outside of marriage. Murray assumes a causal connection, with boys born to unmarried mothers growing up to be *"essentially barbarians."* A key assumption in Murray's thought is **that males are only civilised by marriage** and without the pressure to marry (which the Welfare State removes) they turn to drugs and crime. This is how the **Underclass** is created.

In 1989, Murray visited the UK and wrote an article for *The Sunday Times* in which he argued that Britain has a *"nascent* (meaning 'only just born') *Underclass."* Ten years later he followed up the research and concluded that the UK Underclass had become the same as the American one, just as he had previously warned: young males dropping out of the workforce, births to unmarried mothers rising, violent crime rising.

Murray's argument rests on a **statistical correlation** (worklessness, violent crime, illegitimate births) but correlations never prove cause-and-effect. Moreover, his ideas do not explain the **Great Crime Decline** (p95) but they are supported by research into the social backgrounds of violent offenders (p101).

Melanie Phillips (1999) is a **Right Realist** (p123) who argues that most of the problems Murray complains about originate in the upper classes, who started the trend for divorce and cohabitation (living together without marrying) and drug-taking before these habits spread to the working classes, saying *"that culture was created by our élites."* Phillips argues we must restore incentives for people to marry, not punish vulnerable people who make mistakes.

Right Realism

Another Perspective to emerge in the 1980s was **Realism**. Realists jettison the highly theoretical aspects of Consensus and Conflict Theory and focus on the more practical elements. **Right Realism** takes basic Functionalist ideas, but abandons concepts like value consensus, boundary maintenance and anomie. However, it keeps the focus on **individual responsibility**, the importance of **socialisation** and the insight that **people will behave badly unless society gives them a reason not to**.

Cornish & Clarke (1986) propose a **Rational Choice Theory** of crime. They claim that individuals engage in crime when opportunities present themselves and there seems to be little risk (a lack of **social control**, p77). Cornish & Clarke believe that criminals make rational decisions when deciding when to commit a crime or not. They cite burglary as an example: burglars ask themselves questions like, *Which house offers the best target? Do the neighbours watch out for each other? How hard will it be to gain entrance? What sorts of goods are inside? How will I get out in a hurry? What chance of success do I have?*

This means crime can be prevented by 'hardening' targets (p137), increasing the likelihood of being caught or increasing the severity of punishment to make the crime not worth the risk.

Right Realism is very similar to the **New Right** (p122) in its attitudes and many Right Realists accept Murray's concept of the **Underclass**. However, Right Realists believe crime needs to be solved by more practical methods than cutting benefits or penalising single parent families.

RESEARCH PROFILE: WILSON (1975)

James Q Wilson (1975) pioneered the Right Realist approach in his book ***Thinking About Crime* (1975)**. Wilson takes the view that factors like family structure, unemployment and cultural attitudes to marriage are impossible to control, so it's not worth focusing on them. He points out that most poor people are law-abiding so poverty cannot be the cause of crime.

Wilson claims that crime is linked to a breakdown in **social order** (p77). Disorder in neighbourhoods causes a loss of a sense of community, a decline in **informal social control** and this breeds crime. Wilson believes that architecture affects the way people behave: if you are surrounded by damaged and run-down buildings, you see this as an excuse to commit crime.

This means crime can be prevented by improving the physical environment of our cities: removing graffiti and litter and challenging those who produce it as well as designing streets and buildings to encourage neighbours to feel a sense of community.

Wilson also argues that crime is reduced by enforcing the law (similar to the **Rational Choice Theory** of crime, p123). However, Wilson argues that severe punishments aren't as important as the **certainty of detection**: if punishments are severe but the likelihood of being caught is low, offenders will gamble on getting away with it; if the likelihood of being caught is high, offenders will be deterred even if the punishments are mild.

Research: revisit your notes on **1A; Socialisation, Culture & Identity** and link these ideas to **Wilson & Kelling**'s idea of '**Broken Windows**' and **Zero Tolerance Policing**: can you see now why these are Right Realist ideas? And yes, the 'Wilson' of Wilson & Kelling is **James Q Wilson**.

AO2 ILLUSTRATION: THE COLUMBINE SCHOOL SHOOTINGS

In 1999, **Eric Harris and Dylan Klebold**, two American teenagers, went into **Columbine High School, Colorado** armed with shotguns and home-made bombs. They killed 13 people (12 of their fellow students and one teacher) and wounded 20 more and would have harmed more people if their bombs had gone off successfully. Both gunmen shot themselves after the police arrived.

Harris and Klebold were considered outsiders by their peers because of their **Goth** fashion (wearing long black trench coats). They left behind homemade videotapes in which they showed their plans, methods and practising with guns. The pair had a love for violent video games (e.g. *Doom*) and gloomy rock music (e.g. Marilyn Manson) and an obsession with death and guns that appeared in their school work. They came from conventional and loving families.

Consensus sociologists find a lot of support in mass shootings like this, where the killers are isolated misfits who are not integrated into society and suffer from **anomie**. The fact that they belong to a violent subculture hostile to society is significant too. However, Harris and Klebold were not from the **Underclass**; they were products of exactly the sort of healthy nuclear families that **Functionalists** and the **New Right** endorse. They carried out their attacks while being recorded by CCTV cameras, which is a problem for the **Right Realist** view.

Research: find out about other school shootings and relate them to Consensus theories; watch Michael Moore's documentary *Bowling For Columbine* (2002)

CONFLICT PERSPECTIVE: MARXISM

Marxists don't accept that crime comes from being badly socialised and they certainly don't agree that there's something inherently deviant about being working class.

Instead, Marxists argue that Capitalism itself is **criminogenic** – it is a system that creates crime and drives people to commit crime. **Young (1984)** claims we live in a 'bulimic society' where the constant need to get the latest products, brands and fashions causes people to become deranged.

For Marxists, the real criminals are the rulers of the Capitalist system and they argue that the **White Collar Crime** carried out by corporations does far more damage to society than muggers or hooligans on the streets.

However, **ruling class ideology** (especially as it is presented through the **Media**) causes people to focus on the wrong things. People have an exaggerated fear of street crime and working class youths, but dismiss white collar crime as harmless or unimportant. The police crack down on working class youths, but don't pursue white collar criminals; this is called **selective enforcement**.

This can be explained by **Althusser (1970)** who identifies the **Ideological State Apparatus** (ISA, e.g. the Media) and the **Repressive State Apparatus** (RSA, e.g. the police) which combine to support Capitalism.

Research: revisit your notes on *1A: Socialisation, Culture & Identity* and link these ideas to *Jock Young*, *Edwin Sutherland* and *Louis Althusser*.

Traditional Marxists are sceptical about working class crime and in the past tended to dismiss it as a fiction created by the news media to justify the use of the police and demonise the working classes. Over time, this view has become less credible and most Marxists today accept that working class crime is real, but they tend to insist that the **white collar crimes** of the wealthy are just as important or more so.

RESEARCH PROFILE: GORDON (1971)

David M Gordon (1971) wrote *Class & the Economics of Crime* **(1971)** in which he says that Capitalist societies are *"dog eat dog societies"* in which each individual is encouraged to look out for their own interests before anyone else's, including the wider community and the environment. Capitalism encourages us to be greedy and teaches us that it is acceptable to harm others in pursuit of our selfish desires. This is the basis of crime.

Gordon argues that the police focus attention on working class areas and the criminal justice system (CJS) focuses on prosecuting working class criminals. The CJS ignores the crimes of the wealthy, although they are just as likely (or more) to commit crime as the working classes.

Selective law enforcement (p92) benefits the Capitalist system in three major ways: **(1)** by punishing individuals and making an example of them as *'social failures'* it covers up the flaws in society (inequality and poverty) that create the conditions which lead to crime; **(2)** oppressing the working classes neutralises the only people motivated to resist ruling class dominance; **(3)** imprisoning criminals hides away *"worst jetsam of Capitalist society"* so the rest of us do not see the real human cost of Capitalism.

Gordon's ideas are echoed by **Holdaway**'s study of police occupational culture (p88) and **Jock Young**'s concept of **social bulimia** (p125).

Neo-Marxism / Radical Criminology

Neo means 'new' and **Neo-Marxism** emerged in the 1970s as update of Marxist thought. A big inspiration was **Antonio Gramsci (1891-1937)** who moved away from the idea of a revolution to overthrow Capitalism. Gramsci observed that the ruling class was no longer a literal class of aristocrats and factory owners, but had become a **Hegemony**, a confederation of influential people with a vested interest in keeping Capitalism going. Gramsci pointed out that Hegemony **'manufactures consent'** through education and the Media.

Neo-Marxists take the basic Marxist idea that Capitalism is **criminogenic** and the laws are **selectively enforced** to benefit the ruling class, but they add insights from **Interactionism** (especially **Labelling Theory**, p84) that the rulers have the power to **label marginalised groups** as deviant and that people can **internalise** this label, viewing themselves that way (the **Self-Fulfilling Prophecy**).

Neo-Marxists therefore recognise that working class people do in fact commit crime – the **official crime statistics** (p87) do describe something real. However, for Neo-Marxists it is important to understand **why** working class crime occurs. It is a form of **resistance** to Capitalism. Resistance falls short of revolution. Crime is not an attempt to overthrow Capitalism, but it is a **symbolic** statement of opposition and non-consent to hegemonic values. It is a way for working class people to protest the system and the inequalities in their lives.

This comes very close to a **Functionalist** argument, that crime is a way of venting frustration and signalling dysfunction. However, Neo-Marxists argue crime needs to be understood as a symbol or a ritual; it is not just a protest demanding more rights or more money but rather it is a coded way of wishing to dismantle the entire Capitalist system.

Meanwhile, Neo-Marxists continue to assert that the **white collar crime** of the ruling class is far more damaging than the petty street crime of the working classes and that the police and the news media combine to focus on working class crime, almost to the exclusion of anything else. Neo-Marxist arguments like this appear in **Hall**'s *Policing The Crisis* (p99).

RESEARCH PROFILE: TAYLOR, WALTON & YOUNG (1972)

Ian Taylor, Paul Walton & Jock Young (yes, him again!) wrote *The New Criminology* (1972) in which they present a *"radical theory of crime"* – hence their approach is sometimes called **radical criminology** (and appears as this in the OCR Specification, so make sure you revise this bit!) but you will also see it called **critical criminology**.

They argue for a *"fully social theory of deviance"* which considers the way a Capitalist society is structured (just like any Marxist criminology) but also the motives of the individuals involved (that's the *"radical"* bit). They don't just mean the motives of the offenders (that would be what **Subcultural Theory** already does) but also the motives of the police and judges involved.

Radical Criminology focuses on three aspects of a crime: (**1**) the **circumstances** surrounding the choice to commit the crime (e.g. poverty, discrimination, lack of education – standard Marxist focus on inequality); (**2**) the **meaning of the act** for the individual; (**3**) the **societal reaction**, including **labelling** and **deviancy amplification** (based on **Interactionism**, p131).

Radical Criminologists contend that the *meaning of the act* is not usually to gain money or hurt someone; rather it is to resist Capitalism: it is meant to be a symbolic act of defiance.

Critics of Radical Criminology point out that very few crimes have a clear political meaning to them; most are much more straightforwardly about getting money or settling scores. However, unlike **Strain Theory** (p120), Radical Criminology is quite good at explaining **non-utilitarian** crime, like violence, arson, vandalism and graffiti. **Left Realists** (including Jock Young himself, a decade later) criticise Radical Criminology for painting working class criminals as 'Robin Hood' figures and ignoring the harm they do to their (usually working class) victims.

Left Realism

Right Realism emerged in the 1980s but another Realist Perspective emerged to answer it: **Left Realism**. Left Realists jettison the highly theoretical aspects of Conflict Theory and focus on the more practical elements. **Left Realism** takes basic Marxist ideas but abandons concepts like resistance to Capitalism (which was so important for **Neo Marxism**, p126). However, it keeps the focus on **Capitalism being criminogenic**, the importance of **selective policing** and the insight that **people will behave well unless society gives them a reason not to**.

Jock Young (1986) terms the earlier types of Marxist criminologists (including his own **radical criminology**) as 'Left Idealists.' He argues that Left Realists must steer a path between two extremes: on the one hand the **New Right** who are hysterical about the **Underclass** (p122) and want to over-police marginalised communities; on the other hand the Left Idealists who are in denial about the negative impact of crime on the most vulnerable people in society.

For example, the **Islington Crime Survey** (p90) was crucial in supporting the Left Realist view, because it showed people in a very deprived neighbourhood – especially women – suffering a 'curfew' because of the realistic fear of crime.

Left Realism involves being tough on crime, but also tough on the causes of crime. It's a two-pronged approach, which involves using the police to detect and punish criminals, but making sure they police communities fairly, and also alleviating the poverty and inequality that makes crime attractive for people in those communities.

By acknowledging working class criminality, Left Realism could be criticised for abandoning the strict defence of the working class of earlier Marxism and giving credibility to moral panics in the news media. However, it has been immensely influential, especially in the Labour Government of 1997-2010, and has had more political results than any other type of Marxist criminology.

RESEARCH PROFILE: LEA & YOUNG (1984)

John Lea & Jock Young (again!) wrote *What's To Be Done About Law & Order?* **(1984)** in which they make the case for Left Realism. There are three key concepts: **relative deprivation**, **marginalisation** and **subculture**.

Lea & Young argue that crime is caused by deprivation, but deprivation itself is not directly responsible for crime; they admit that deprivation has fallen since the austerity of the 1950s but crime has gone up. **Relative deprivation** refers to how someone feels compared to other people or their own expectations. Although people are better off today, they have a feeling of relative deprivation because advertising has raised expectations for material possessions – we are wealthier, but we feel poorer. This creates a pressure to keep up with expectations, which leads to crime. This idea influenced **Jock Young**'s theory of **social bulimia** (p125).

Marginalisation is where people cannot participate fully in society. Marginalised groups lack organisations to represent their interests and clear goals. For example, workers have groups to represent them (e.g. trade unions) and clear goals (e.g. better pay) so they don't need to resort to crime. Marginalised groups (e.g. the unemployed or youth) have no clear goals and no one representing them, so they turn to crime in frustration.

A group's collective response to relative deprivation and marginalisation is to form a **subculture** – this is similar to **Cohen's theory of status frustration** (p121). There are **subcultural adaptations** to the problems that groups face and not all involve crime (e.g. some marginalised groups become very religious). However, some subcultures retain the mainstream cultural goal of acquiring wealth but lack the resources to achieve it and these are at risk of becoming criminal subcultures – this is similar to **Merton's Strain Theory** (p120).

Lea & Young argue that crime is caused by lots of different factors (termed a **multiple aetiology**) so it is important to understand why people offend, what shapes public attitudes and responses to crime and the factors that influence the police. They propose that an effective community should work *together* to solve crime.

AO2 ILLUSTRATION: THE MACPHERSON REPORT (1999)

Four years after the murder of **Stephen Lawrence** in 1993 (p106), a Government Inquiry was set up to look into the way the Metropolitan Police had handled the case. Sir William Macpherson chaired the investigation, and the **'Stephen Lawrence Inquiry'** is known as the **Macpherson Report**, which was published in 1999. It ran to 350 pages and contained 70 recommendations. Macpherson concluded that the police investigation into Stephen Lawrence's death had been *"marred by a combination of professional incompetence, institutional racism and a failure of leadership"* Officers in the Metropolitan police were named and shamed and the entire force was criticised.

Following the report, the Metropolitan Police introduced targets to recruit and promote Black and Asian officers and the **Independent Police Complaints Commission** was set up to monitor the police.

Macpherson defines **institutional racism** as *"the collective failure of an organisation to provide an appropriate and professional service to people because of their colour, culture or ethnic origin."* The point about institutional racism is that it is based on the way an organisation works, so the individuals in it might not be personally racist, but they will act as if they were just by following the organisation's rules and procedures.

The Macpherson Report is strong support for **Neo-Marxist** and **Left Realist** ideas about **selective policing** (p92); it backs up the findings of **Holdaway** (p88) and **Fitzgerald's Policing For London Survey** (p107) and continues to inform the debate about **Stop & Search** targeting Black people.

CONFLICT PERSPECTIVE: FEMINISM

Feminists don't offer an explanation of all crime everywhere. Instead, they challenge stereotypes about women and draw attention to crimes committed against women and the unfair way they are treated by the criminal justice system (CJS).

For example, the **Chivalry Thesis** (p104) claims that women are treated better by the CJS, which is why there are fewer arrests or convictions for women. On the face of it, this is supported by **self-report studies** (p91) that show offending rates for males and females are much closer than the huge gulf found in **official crime statistics** (p87). **Frances Heidensohn (1985)** explains it is more complex than this: women who show conventionally feminine behaviour (crying, showing love for their children) may be treated leniently, but those who do not conform to expectations of femininity are treated more harshly.

When it comes to victimisation, **Sandra Walklate (1995)** found female rape victims face a tough rather than chivalrous court system; women who are raped are often not believed and have to prove their respectability before their accusation is taken seriously.

Adler's Liberation Thesis (p105) predicts more women will get involved in crime and this might be proved by the emergence of a **'Ladette' Subculture** in the 1990s and 2000s. However, most Feminists contend that women's crimes are driven, not by liberation, but by poverty and oppression, for example **prostitution** (which is the *only* crime where females outnumber males).

Prostitution and sex work have created a division in Feminism. The **2nd Wave Feminists** of the 1960s and '70s viewed prostitution as exploitation of women by men and many Feminists continue to view it this way. The **4th Wave Feminists** of the 21st century adopt a more **sex-positive** view, arguing that the real problem is that attitude of shame and judgement about women's bodies. Feminists like **Priscilla Alexander (1997)** argue that **sex work** (they do not call it 'prostitution') can be liberating for women and instead of being driven underground it should be legalised, regulated and made safe. The term **'whorephobic'** is sometimes used to attack Feminists who oppose sex work. However, **Julie Bindel (2017)** describes prostitution as *"paid rape"* saying *"if 'consent' has to be bought, it is not consent."*

Sex Work Is Work (photo: SG ZA)

RESEARCH PROFILE: SMART (1976)

Carol Smart wrote *Women, Crime & Criminology* (1976) which had a big impact on the up-till-that-point male world of criminology. She explains that women remain "*invisible*" in male-dominated criminology, and particularly their victimisation is ignored.

Smart suggests that biological differences between sexes aren't an important factor in causing crime. She argues that there is stricter **socialisation** of girls than boys within the family. Parents control how often girls go out, where to and with whom. Girls learn to share exaggerated fears about their safety, even though stranger attacks are rare and boys are far more likely to be victims of violence. This leads to girls and later women becoming prisoners in their own homes.

Women offenders are perceived as **doubly deviant** because they not only break the law but also transgress their gender role, which is to be subordinate and obedient. This is the *opposite* of the **Chivalry Thesis**, but it ties in with **Heidensohn**'s point about women who fail to conform to gender expectations being treated more harshly.

SOCIAL ACTION PERSPECTIVE: INTERACTIONISM

Interactionists reject the sort of structuralist explanations presented so far, like the idea that entire classes of people are behaving a certain way because of social forces.

This approach uses the idea of **societal reaction**. Society (with the help of the news media) picks on a few unconnected cases of people behaving in a deviant way. These cases really have nothing to do with each other, but the media pulls them together in an **ideological framework** (an 'explanation that makes sense'), giving the phenomenon a title like 'crime wave.' All the people involved in it that are now labelled 'criminals.'

Edwin Lemert (1967) points out a distinction between **primary and secondary deviance**.

- **Primary deviance** is something everybody does: we've all stolen things (if only pens from the office or towels from the hotel), broken the law, damaged things that don't belonged to us, had romantic interactions with someone we shouldn't, used obscene language or been violent. Most of the time it goes unnoticed and there are no consequences.
- **Secondary deviance** is deviance that society reacts to. Someone 'calls it out' and assigns a label: we are blamed, accused; people are shocked; the authorities step in. This includes being labelled as a criminal (or a 'thug' or a a 'slut'). At first this label doesn't conform to our self-image and that leads to anxiety. Eventually, we alter our self-image to conform to the label: this is the **Self-Fulfilling Prophecy (SFP)**.

Some labels have **Master Status** and are particularly hard to negotiate or remove. If you are labelled as 'lazy' you can negotiate that label (*'I'm only lazy with subjects I don't enjoy'*) or prove it wrong. If you are labelled as a criminal. It's hard to negotiate (it's no good saying you're not a criminal because you only steal from rich people) or remove – the label can stick for years. Since young people have less power in society, it's harder for them to avoid secondary deviance or negotiate deviant labels.

Howard Becker (1963) applies the idea of societal reaction to marijuana smokers. He argues that drug-users have to learn from others how to take a drug. When agencies of social control 'clamp down,' users start to see themselves as drug-users (rather than just friends with a similar pastime): they accept their **deviant label** and the drug becomes central to their lifestyle. In this way, attempts to prevent drug-use end up creating, rather than preventing, drug-addicts.

Research: revisit your notes on **1A: Socialisation, Culture & Identity** and link these ideas to **Howard Becker's** *Outsiders*

Critics say that secondary deviance is only a good explanation of delinquency and non-serious crime; it's hard to argue that murder is only regarded as criminal because society labels it that way. It's also hard to see how labelling can explain hidden crimes like child abuse.

Interactionism is accused of being a ***description*** of crime rather than an ***explanation***. For example, why does society single out certain individuals or groups in the first place? where does the ideological framework tying these behaviours together come from? why does the news media stir up outrage rather than, say, curiosity or admiration?

Neo-Marxists like **Stuart Hall** (**1978**, p99) claim to have the answer to this: the Media has a structural relationship to Capitalist institutions, so it regularly scapegoats marginalised groups to blame them for crises in Capitalism.

RESEARCH PROFILE: CHAMBLISS (1973)

In 1973, **William Chambliss** published *The Saints & the Roughnecks*, an article describing two years spent observing Hannibal High School students (age 16-19) in America. He followed two gangs: six working class Roughnecks and eight middle class Saints. (The names of the gangs and the school are fictional to protect the anonymity of the boys and their families).

Chambliss observes that the Saints' behaviour was in many ways ***worse*** than the Roughnecks, engaging in truancy, under-age drinking, dangerous driving and vandalism. Yet they were seen as model students, whereas the Roughnecks were constantly in trouble with teachers and police.

The Saints were successful in school, viewed as 'good students' by the teachers and found it easy to truant by pretending to have extracurricular activities. Since they had cars, they could travel to other suburbs or into the city to misbehave, where no one would recognise them. When they got into trouble with the police, they could pay fines and their parents would vouch for them.

The Roughnecks were viewed as delinquents. Their truancy was lower than the Saints, but it was public knowledge. Without cars, they had to gather in their own neighbourhood, where their fighting and drunkenness was observed. There were in trouble with the police and, while Chambliss observed them, each Roughneck was arrested at least once.

Chambliss uses **Labelling Theory** to explain his findings: the Saints had positive labels so their behaviour was interpreted as harmless; the Roughnecks were interpreted as delinquent because of their negative labels. The Saints went on to college and good jobs. The Roughnecks had different outcomes: attempted suicide, prison, gambling, unemployment.

Chambliss connects this to a **Marxist** understanding of class and privilege. Social control is imposed on the working classes, but not the middle classes, and this control *creates* deviancy rather than reducing it.

Chambliss' study is from the 1970s and the USA, so the results might not apply to 21st century criminals or the UK, where teenagers don't drive until they are 18 but they can legally buy alcohol before they are 21. The boys were white, so the study doesn't tell us about other ethnic groups or girls. The small sample size, although typical of **Interactionist** research, is hard to generalise from: these could have been unusual teenagers at an unusual school.

*Chambliss is a **Neo-Marxist** so his research could be used to support that Perspective (p126). The Saints' ability to negotiate with the police and avoid detection can be used to analyse **social class patterns & trends** (p101).*

Research: review your notes for **1A: Socialisation, Culture & Identity** to link this study to **Willis'** *Learning To Labour* (1973) where 'the Lads' behave similarly to Chambliss' Roughnecks (although they are a year or two younger). It is also interesting to compare with the Spur Posse observed by **Faludi** in *Stiffed* (1991).

AO2 ILLUSTRATION: ONLYFANS BANS PORN

OnlyFans (OF) is a subscriber website that features content creators offering recipes and yoga instruction but is mainly famous for porn. *OF* has tens of thousands of sex workers who hand over 20% of their earnings to the site – but in 2021 *OF* announced it would ban pornographic content. This led to sex workers on the site claiming it was destroying their livelihoods. Defenders argue that sex work online is safer for women and enables them to be their own bosses. Critics point out that women are scammed, stalked and trolled on the site and the site owners do not listen to the complaints of women who are abused by their 'fans.'

OF is a good example of the **debate about sex work within Feminism** (p130), but also the way in which female deviancy is treated differently from male deviancy (the idea of **relativity** and **social construction**) since *OF* is closing down businesses that are not actually illegal and which are largely carried out by women. The term 'sex worker' is an attempt to **negotiate a different label**, because 'prostitute' has **master status**.

EXAM PRACTICE: EXPLAINING CRIME & DEVIANCE

The OCR exam has three questions in **Paper 3 Section B**. Questions 7-9 are on Education and questions 10-12 are on Religion, Belief & Faith, but this Study Guide is focused on **Option 1** which covers questions **4-6**:

4. In what ways is does Feminism explain gender differences in offending? **[10 marks: 6 AO1 + 4 AO2]**

This is one of those 'describe & illustrate' questions, but with no Source A or Source B to lean on. No need to evaluate.

Make two sociological points about Feminism and gender differences –a point about male offending and a point about female offending. It's a good idea to refer to particular statistics (like 80% of crime being male) and you should definitely use some sociological terminology (like socialisation, the invisibility of women and the Chivalry Thesis). Then offer examples of crimes and make sure each example has an explanation. For example, "Females are more involved in crime than they were, such as the rise of Ladette culture."

5. To what extent is the New Right a good explanation of social class differences in offending? **[20 marks: 8 AO1 + 4 AO2 + 8 AO3]**

This is a mid-size essay with a requirement for developed evaluation. You should spend 25 minutes and write at least 500 words.

*Write **three** points. Each point should introduce a sociological idea with some illustration from the real world. Each point should finish off with a developed evaluation (see **Chapter 9** for this). For example, you could write about the benefits trap, single parent families and violent young males. Make sure you mention **Murray**'s research and be sure to answer the question: is the New Right a good explanation or not?*

6. Outline and evaluate radical criminology as an explanation of crime and deviance. **[40 marks: 16 AO1 + 8 AO2 + 16 AO3]**

This is the last of the two big (40 mark) essays in OCR A-Level Sociology. You should spend 50 minutes and write at least 1000 words.

*Write **five** points. Each point should introduce a sociological idea with some illustration from the real world. Each point should finish off with a developed evaluation (see **Chapter 9** for this). For example, you could write about Neo-Marxism being different from traditional Marxism, the importance of Interactionism, the idea of pre-crime circumstances, the motive for the act and post-crime labelling. Make a point of mentioning **Taylor et al**'s book **The New Criminology** but don't forget about **Hall** and **Chambliss** too. Be sure to come to a conclusion: is radical criminology the best explanation or was Left Realism a better replacement?*

CHAPTER 8 – REDUCING CRIME & DEVIANCE

The OCR Specification asks '*How can crime and deviance be reduced?*' and it goes on to define "*reduced*" as **prevention**, **punishment** and **control**:

- **Prevention** means strategies that make crime and deviance less likely to occur in the first place. This includes punishments that are so frightening that people don't dare misbehave (**deterrence**) as well as things to make misbehaviour harder or less appealing.
- **Punishment** means strategies to respond to a crime after it has occurred. Punishment can make someone less likely to reoffend (**reformation**) because the punishment was so awful no one would want to go through it again. Punishment can be **retribution**, enforcing the values of the law-abiding community, or **reparation**, which is getting the offender to repair the damage they have caused.
- **Control** means changing people so that they don't misbehave in future. It can involve rehabilitating offenders to make them into better citizens or just monitoring them closely, so they find it more difficult to re-offend (**protection** of the public).

These strategies are part of **social policy**, which means the actions taken by the police, the courts, social services (like youth workers) and laws passed by the government to reduce crime and deviance.

Because social policy involves politics, you need to understand an important political distinction.

Right Wing politics

Right Wing politics are inspired by **Consensus Theory** in sociology and are represented in the UK by the **Conservative Party**. Right Wing views favour traditional institutions (family, church, the Royal Family) and tend to be nationalistic. They prefer gradual reform and are suspicious of revolutionary change. They prefer power to be located close to communities (e.g. at a town council or parish level) and are suspicious of 'Big Government' and giving more power to the state – and especially to international organisations like the EU and UN. Right Wingers value marriage and work and are suspicious of benefits and anything that seems to reward laziness or irresponsibility.

Right Wing Views on Crime Reduction

It is a Right Wing idea that **people will behave badly unless society gives them a reason not to**. This means humans will be violent, selfish and criminal unless something restrains them from behaving that way – and what restrains them is **social order** (p77), which means pressure from their family and community and an awareness of the risks of breaking the rules. People are individually responsible for their crimes and you can't shift the blame to poverty, inequality or the structure of society.

On a society-wide level, crime is best reduced by making sure people are in work and living as part of a healthy family unit. Young men in particular need to be socialised by discipline from parents and later by responsibilities in a marriage. Strong communities keep crime in check.

On a more local level, people need to be watched. The anonymity of living in a big city encourages crime but having architecture that lets neighbours see what's going on and gives troublemakers nowhere to hide reduces this problem.

People are rational when it comes to crime, so if you make the risks outweigh the benefits crime will reduce. This means tough punishments for crime and visible police presence – or else CCTV cameras that assure people they won't get away with crime.

Left Wing politics

Left Wing politics are inspired by **Conflict Theory** in sociology and are represented in the UK by the **Labour Party** and the **Green Party** and (to a lesser extent) the **Liberal Democrats**. Left Wing views regard traditional institutions as unhelpful and out-of-date; they tend to be international in outlook and suspicious of nationalism. They prefer sweeping changes over gradual reform. They regard 'Big Government' as a powerful ally in bringing about social change. Left Wingers are concerned for the marginalised people in society – the poor, ethnic minority groups, LGBT minorities, etc. – and believe the majority should make sacrifices to benefit these minorities, such as taxing the wealthy to fund the Welfare State.

Left Wing Views on Crime Reduction

It is a Left Wing idea that **people will behave well unless society gives them a reason not to**. This means humans will only be violent, selfish and criminal if society forces them to behave this way – and what forces them to do this is poverty, discrimination and frustration at being excluded. People are not necessarily individually responsible for their crimes and you can't blame the criminal without taking into account the circumstances that produced him or her.

On a society-wide level, crime is best reduced by making sure people are more equal and fully included in society. Discrimination based on race, gender, religion or background needs to be challenged. More money needs to be spent benefiting deprived communities.

On a more local level, people need to be consulted. The police need to work *with* local communities, not *against* them, and the makeup of the police force should match the demographics of the society they police (e.g. in terms of ethnicity).

Criminals are in some sense victims too, so being tough on them only brutalises them and makes them more hostile. Sentences need to focus on rehabilitating people so they can rejoin society and play a constructive role in future.

Research: revisit your notes on **Section A** and combine these ideas with the details about the Culture Wars (p46) and Social Justice (p53) – and in **1A: Socialisation, Culture & Identity** you can link this to the debate over Defunding The Police.

REDUCING CRIME & DEVIANCE: A TOOLKIT

The OCR Specification expects you to be able to discuss Right Wing and Left Wing approaches to reducing crime in detail. These approaches are:

Left Wing	Right Wing
Community crime prevention & punishment	Situational & environmental crime prevention
Restorative Justice	Retributive justice
Structural changes in society	Punitive punishment & control

We will consider Right Wing approaches first as they are more representative of the political approach in the UK today and over the last decade or more.

SITUATIONAL & ENVIRONMENTAL CRIME PREVENTION

Ronald Clarke (1983) discusses five aspects of crime prevention: (**1**) **increase effort** of crime, such as using locks, screens and barriers between the criminal and their target; (**2**) **increase risk** of being caught, including street lighting, security guards and Neighbourhood Watch schemes; (**3**) **reduce rewards** of crime by hiding valuable goods, moving away from cash and fitting ink tags that ruin stolen goods; (**4**) **reduce provocations**, such as segregating hostile fans at sports matches, reducing crowding in pubs and banning violent pornography; (**5**) **remove excuses** by making the rules clear, such as through obvious signs ('No Parking') and roadside displays that inform motorists of their speed.

Situational crime prevention is also known as **target hardening**. It involves making crime more difficulty, inconvenient or risky in specific situations. Classic examples are burglar alarms on houses and central locking on cars, PINs on mobile phones and electromagnetic tags on shop goods like clothes or alcohol (those plastic clips the shop assistant removes when you buy them and set off an alarm if you leave with them).

If criminals are rational, these strategies make crime a less attractive choice: **effort is increased** and **rewards are reduced**. They are also mostly used by businesses or private individuals, so they don't involve extending the reach of Big Government into people's private lives, which is good from a Right Wing viewpoint.

Environmental crime prevention is about making sure an entire area (like a tower block, an estate or a city street) is constructed in a way that deters crime. This includes things like street lighting and designing homes to give neighbours a view outside their property so they see people coming and going. This **increases risk** and **reduces provocation and excuses**.

Clarke includes **surveillance** in this category, particularly CCTV cameras. Right Wing critics are less keen on CCTV, since it infringes on individual privacy.

AO2 ILLUSTRATION: FACIAL RECOGNITION TECHNOLOGY

There are at least 5 million CCTV cameras in the UK, which is one for every 13 people – however 96% are owned by householders or businesses and only 4% are owned by the state (source: **CCTV.co.uk**).

New **automatic facial recognition (AFR)** technology allows such cameras to access databases and identify people walking or driving past. China has invested heavily in AFR, but there is opposition in Western countries, based on civil liberties and the right to privacy.

In 2020, the UK Court of Appeal ruled that South Wales Police's use of AFR was *"unlawful"* and the EU is considering banning AFR in public places.

Police forces must have a reason to use this technology (rather than just 'fishing' through public places) and a human officer must double-check identifications made (since the technology is alleged to be biased towards identifying White faces accurately).

RESEARCH PROFILE: NEWMAN (1972)

City planner **Oscar Newman** wrote *Defensible Space* **(1972)** in which he argues that architecture can reduce crime. Newman studies a New York tower block and a low-rise estate with similar levels of deprivation but found crime was higher in the tower block, where residents could not look out onto their own gardens or monitor who was coming or going in the building. In particular, gangs vandalised the lifts and occupied the stairwells where they were out of sight but could menace passers-by.

Newman defines defensible space as *"a residential environment whose physical characteristics – building layout and site plan – function to allow inhabitants themselves to become key agents in ensuring their security."* He argues that humans are naturally territorial and want to monitor their territory and make it secure. Housing should exploit this tendency for the mutual benefit of all the residents, so that people take responsibility for their surroundings.

Newman was an architect not a sociologist, but his ideas mirror the **Right Realist** (p123) focus on the importance of surveillance and the reduction of anonymity to prevent crime. However, his conclusions have been criticised because not all projects built according to his ideas have shown reduced crime and even when they do the reasons might be something other than territoriality (such as better jobs and opportunities around a new housing development).

RETRIBUTIVE JUSTICE

Retributive justice is the idea that the punishment should fit the crime and reflect the values of the community: the offender should experience the outrage of the entire community they have wronged, not just their specific victim. It is important for **boundary maintenance** (p77).

Retributive punishment tends to involve lengthy **custodial sentences** (meaning prison sentences) and it is proposed that this deters people from offending and causes prisoners to think twice about re-offending. However, with 47% of prisoners re-offending within a year of being released (source: **Prison Reform Trust, 2013**), this justification is contested. **Right Realists** maintain that the reason prison does not deter is because it is in fact too 'soft.'

Another argument for retributive justice is that it enables the offender to experience moral growth. 'Softer' punishments only delude convicts into thinking that their offence was not really so serious, which cheats them of self-knowledge and the opportunity to turn themselves around. Left Realist **John Braithwaite (1989)** called this **disintegrative shaming** and argues that **restorative justice** (p145) is what leads to personal change. The Interactionist **Howard Garfinkel (1956)** calls them **degradation ceremonies** and argues they apply negative labels to people.

The ultimate form of retributive justice is **capital punishment** (the death penalty). This is based on the idea that the value of a life in society can be measured by the punishment given to someone who takes a life, so execution is the only fair punishment for a murderer. The death penalty still exists in (as of 2021) 24 out of 50 US States but was abolished in the UK in 1965 (1973 in Northern Ireland). Of course, capital punishment does *not* permit an offender to grow in moral self-knowledge (unless there's an afterlife).

Not all **Right Realists** agree with retributive justice; **James Q Wilson** (p124) argues that certainty of being detected is more effective at reducing crime than the harshness of the punishment.

AO2 ILLUSTRATION: THREE STRIKES & YOU'RE OUT

In 1994, the USA introduced **habitual offender laws**, which were nicknamed **'Three Strikes Laws'** based on the phrase used in baseball to describe a hitter being declared 'out' after three swings and misses. The laws (which vary from State to State) means that the third time a person is convicted of a serious crime, the judge has no choice but give a long custodial (prison) sentence.

An example is from 2009 when a Leonard Andrade stole $153 worth of videotapes from a K-Mart store. He had previous convictions for drugs and burglary so under California's 'Three Strikes Law' he was sentenced to 50 years in prison with no chance of parole.

This illustrates a fierce debate over 'Three Strikes Laws.' Defenders claim the punishment deters criminals and makes the rational choice to commit a third crime very risky. Critics point out that a 50-year sentence for stealing $153 is wildly disproportionate. 'Three Strikes' has been linked to the **McDonaldisation** of punishment (**Ritzer, 1993**) because it makes machine-like efficiency more important than making sure an offender gets the punishment he or she morally deserves.

RESEARCH PROFILE: BECKETT & EVANS (2018)

Katherine Beckett & Heather Evans produced a report on the role of race in capital sentencing for the Washington State Supreme Court in 2018. Based on their findings, the Court then voted to abolish the death penalty after 99 years of use.

Beckett & Evans studied all capital cases in the State from 1981-2014 and found that Black defendants were between 3.5 and 4.6 times more likely to receive a death sentence than non-Black defendants. They found that juries were more than 4 times likely to impose a death sentence for Black defendants. In counties with high Black populations, prosecutors were more likely to request the death penalty and judges to sentence convicted felons to death. The researchers explain this by '**implicit racial bias**,' a psychological term describing the same processes that the **Macpherson Report** terms **institutional racism** (p129). The researchers conclude that *"race-blindness continues to elude us."*

The study illustrates a problem with capital punishment: it is disproportionately applied to marginalised groups even when the police, lawyers and judges are not consciously racist.

PUNITIVE PUNISHMENT & CONTROL

'Punitive' just means 'punishing' so 'punitive punishment' is a bit of a redundant expression. Nonetheless, I take this to refer to punishments and policies of control that make a point of being disproportionately harsh – as opposed to **retributive justice** *(p139) that aims to give offenders the punishment they deserve.*

The perception that prisons are too comfortable and that punishment ought to be punitive is a common theme in Right Wing approaches to crime.

Punitive punishment is seen in the **'Short, Sharp Shock'** approach to punishing young offenders. This policy was introduced in 1979 by Margaret Thatcher's Conservative government. It reformed the old Borstals into Detention Centres for young offenders so that they would no longer be *"holiday camps"* but would instead provide a 3-month long military-style regime with early morning wake-up calls, lots of physical exercise and manual labour and only 30 minutes of conversation allowed between inmates each day.

Critics pointed out that the old Borstals were pretty tough places and hardly 'holiday camps' but the regimes in the new DCs verged on torture. Reoffending rates did not change and the 'Short, Sharp Shock' regime was gradually mellowed, incorporating more opportunities for education and rehabilitation.

Punitive Control includes **Zero Tolerance Policing (ZTP)** which was pioneered in New York in the 1990s. This policy involves increasing the number of police officers on foot on the streets (as opposed to driving around in cars or in their offices) and instructing them to target minor crimes of disorder, such as jaywalking (crossing the road away from a pedestrian crossing, which is illegal in the USA), public drunkenness and urination, littering, graffiti and vandalism.

Within a few years of its introduction in New York, crime had dropped by 30-50% and New York went from being one of the world's most dangerous cities to being one of the safest. However, the period of ZTP in New York coincided with the **Great Crime Decline** (p95) and many other US cities experienced similar drops in crime despite not following the police.

ZTP is based on the **Broken Windows** theory (**Wilson & Kelling, 1982**). This **Right Realist** theory argues that people are influenced by disorder in their environment and are more likely to commit serious crimes if minor crimes seem to be being ignored.

> **Research:** revisit your notes on **1A: Socialisation, Culture & Identity** you can link this to Wilson & Kelling and Broken Windows

AO2 ILLUSTRATION: ZERO TOLERANCE POLICING

ZTP became an official policy in New York under Right Wing Mayor **Rudy Giuliani** who was elected in 1993; during the 1990s the New York homicide rate fell by 82& compared to 53% in other cities. However, it had started falling before Giuliani was elected. **Bill Bratton**, the New York Police Chief, claims that ZTP was successful because it engaged with local communities and tackle the minor crimes that mattered to them, rather than coming down heavily on *all* crimes.

Bratton's analysis makes ZTP sound more like a version of **community crime prevention** (p143).

ZTP has been piloted in the UK in the 1990s, in the King's Cross area of London, Hartlepool, Middlesbrough and Strathclyde. It was championed by **Ray Mallon**, head of Middlesbrough CID, who promised to cut crime by 20% in 18 months using ZTP and achieved this – as he had cut crime by 38% in his previous post in Hartlepool. However, Mallon was suspended for misconduct.

Other than Mallon, ZTP has not been popular with British police forces. Critics claim it creates conflict with minority groups and leads to heavy-handed policing. One of the demands of the **Black Lives Matter** campaigns in 2020 was the end of ZTP in America.

RESEARCH PROFILE: PUNCH (2007)

Maurice Punch analyses attempt to import ZTP by police forces in the UK and the Netherlands.

Punch argues that ZTP under Bratton's leadership in New York really consisted of three different approaches: (**1**) **information-led policing** ("Compstat"), where officers met to analyse crime data and plan strategies; (**2**) "**Fixing Broken Windows**," which meant reclaiming parts of the city, building links with communities and involving business to reverse decline; (**3**) **assertive police presence** on the streets, targeting particular low-level crimes.

Punch contends that British and Dutch observers only adopted the third strategy of assertive policing, without noticing the importance of the other two.

Evaluating Right Wing Views on Crime Reduction

Right Wing views on crime reduction are immensely popular with the general public, who always want the government to 'get tough' on crime.

Situational and **environmental crime prevention** have been immensely successful and might explain much of the **Great Crime Decline** (p95). However, these developments are not really social policies. They are products of new technology that members of the public and businesses have taken advantage of. Remember that only 4% of CCTV cameras in the UK are run by the state? These developments are things that would have happened regardless of which government was in power, Right or Left Wing.

This sort of crime prevention and control also raises concerns, especially about **privacy**. New surveillance technology enables the state to 'snoop' on citizens as they go about their business and **civil liberties campaigners** argue this is a breach of human rights. Right Wing politicians tend to be in favour of privacy and oppose Big Government, so even though **automatic facial recognition technology** might prevent more crime if it were rolled out nationally (e.g. by detecting a wanted offender while they were walking their dog), Right Wingers will not always support it.

The other strand of Right Wing criminology involves getting tough on offenders. Despite **James Q Wilson**'s argument that what matters is preventing crime by making sure offenders know they will be caught, the focus always shifts to making punishments as harsh as possible. A key element in Right Wing thought is always that punishments are currently too soft and that the wrong people (convicted criminals, the **Underclass**, etc.) are having too easy a time.

Much research suggests that making punishments tougher tends to impact disproportionately on marginalised groups, who bear the brunt of heavy-handed policing and tough sentencing (and even the death penalty).

A good example of this is the way **Zero Tolerance Policing** is misrepresented as putting police on the streets and telling them to be aggressive. By itself, this only leads to a deterioration in police relations with communities and stirs up resentment. The other aspects of ZTP, such as **investing in declining neighbourhoods** and **information-led policing**, are not as exciting for the public and are, at the end of the day, policies that Left Wing politicians can support too.

The main criticism of Right Wing approaches is that, by focusing on the control of individual offenders, they neglect the wider social context of crime. They don't try to fix inequality or poverty or challenge discriminatory practices. They don't demand the police reform themselves. They assume that society is fine the way it is and the only motive behind doing crime is an evil nature. Left Wing approaches try to see the bigger picture.

On the other hand, Right Wing approaches do focus on the idea that crime is morally wrong and that it hurts people. The idea that offenders deserve punishment and morally need punishment is an important challenge to the Left Wing view that sees criminals as victims who don't need to change because society is really at fault.

SOCIAL/COMMUNITY CRIME PREVENTION & PUNISHMENT

These strategies are sometimes called an actuarial approach to crime. 'Actuarial' refers to the method used by insurance companies to work out risk, so an actuarial crime prevention strategy works out who is at risk of turning to crime and intervenes to prevent that before it happens. It is based on the idea that crime is not evenly distributed throughout society (*c.f.* **Farrington's Cambridge study** which identifies many risk factors for crime, p110).

Social crime prevention 'targets' particular people or groups for interventions, which could including parenting classes or pre-school lessons or family counselling. They are popular with Left Realists and Neo-Marxists because they address the **pre-crime circumstances** before a crime occurs.

Community crime prevention is an approach particularly associated with America that aims to divert young people from delinquencies by investing in youth clubs, extra lessons and mentoring systems to give at-risk children an older role model (e.g. **Big Brothers Big Sisters of America**).

One community programme that did cross from the USA to the UK in 1982 was the **Neighbourhood Watch** scheme, in which the police assist a street or estate in making their homes more secure, patrolling and reporting suspicious activity. NW schemes often collapse when residents feel the police do not respond to their reports; they work best in areas where residents are homeowners, married with children and over-40: in other words, well-off (source: **Bolton, 2006**).

In many ways, these approaches resemble **situational & environmental crime prevention** (p137), except they are trying to 'tweak' people's social circumstances rather than their physical surroundings.

As with those Right Wing preventative strategies, these are aimed at working class crime and not **white collar crime**. Marxists would argue that, even if these programmes produce improvements in people's living conditions, they don't do anything to tackle the **structural inequality** in in the Capitalist system (p147).

Community punishment is known as **community service** in the UK and was introduced in 1977. It is an alternative to a custodial (prison) sentence for offenders who commit less serious crimes (e.g. criminal damage, fraud, drugs). The court will order between 40-300 hours of community service, often removing graffiti, renovating damaged buildings, litter picking or decorating public places. Unemployed offenders do 3-4 days of service a week; those with jobs must schedule time in their evenings or weekends. **Ministry of Justice (2013)** figures suggest that 35% of offenders on community service reoffend within a year, but that is still 8% better than the reoffending rate for equivalent prison sentences.

One feature of these policies is that they are often endorsed by Right Wing politicians too, which makes you suspect there's nothing specifically Left Wing about them, except for increasing the involvement of the state in people's private lives (which is the only reason Right Wingers object to them).

AO2 ILLUSTRATION: THE TROUBLED FAMILIES PROGRAMME

The Troubled Families Programme (TFP) was set up in 2011 after the riots in British cities that year (p114). The Conservative-led government promised to 'turn around' 120,000 troubled families in order to reduce crime, truancy and other social problems. Families were considered to have 'turned around' if school attendance improved above 85%, youth crime reduced by 33% and anti-social behaviour reduced by 60%; alternatively, if a family member moved off benefits and into employment for 6 months.

The TFP claimed a 99% success rate, but a leaked independent evaluation suggested that it had not had any effect on criminality. Partly this was because the families targeted weren't particularly 'criminal' to begin with.

An interesting feature of the TFP is that you will see it described as a **Left Realist community programme** (it is based on the 'Respect agenda' set up by a previous Labour government) or as a **New Right** policy to get the **Underclass** back into work (p122). It could be seen as *both* of these things, which is a weakness of these policies from a specifically Left Wing viewpoint.

RESEARCH PROFILE: PARKS (1988)

The **Perry Preschool Project** is a famous research study started in 1962 by **David Weikart** in Michigan, USA. This community programme targeted 123 Black American children living in poverty and identified as at risk of educational failure, all age 3-4.

The children were divided randomly into two groups: 58 received the High/Scope pre-school programme from 1962-1967 and 65 children were assigned to a control group. The pre-school activity involved 2½ hour morning sessions in small groups (average child-teacher ratio 6:1). The activities involved decision making and problem solving. There was a weekly 1½ hour home visit to include the mother in the educational process.

According to a project bulletin by **Greg Parks (1999)**, by age 40, the group who received the programme had fewer arrests for violent crime, property crime or drugs; more had graduated from high school and found jobs. It is estimated that for every dollar spent on the programme, $17 was saved on welfare and prison costs.

*This is also an example of an unusual methodology in Sociology: a **longitudinal study** that is also a **field experiment**, comparing an experimental group with a control group.*

RESTORATIVE JUSTICE

Restorative Justice (RJ) brings together the offender and the people harmed by their crime, enabling everyone to play a part in repairing the harm and finding a way forward. In many ways it is the opposite of **retributive justice** (p139), since the focus is on fixing what was broken (including trust and self-estem) instead of making the offender suffer to the same degree as their victim.

The theory of RJ was introduced in **Howard Zehr**'s ground-breaking book *Changing Lenses* **(1990)** which credits the original practice of RJ to the Native Americans and the Maori of New Zealand before the arrival of European settlers. He defines the 'three pillars' of Restorative Justice as:

1. **Harms & Needs:** Who was harmed, what was the harm and how can it be repaired?
2. **Obligations:** Who is responsible how can they repair the harm?
3. **Engagement:** Victims and offenders have active roles in the process

RJ often involves a face-to-face meeting between the offender and the victim – or the victim's family. Alternatively there is indirect communication – for example, if the crime was sexual or violent. Shuttle mediation involves letter-writing or a video-taped message; a proxy is someone else who takes the place of one of the parties in the meeting and relates their responses.

RJ is often used as part of a reduced sentence for the offender or a requirement for a non-custodial sentence (such as doing RJ instead of prison). Sometimes it is used *after* a prison sentence (**probation**) to rehabilitate the prisoner into society. It is always **voluntary**.

RJ is promoted by **Left Realists** (p128). It is based on the theory of the **'Square of Crime'** **(Matthews & Young, 1992)**.

In this view, the interests of various groups intersect in a crime: the offender has harmed the victim and the victim needs redress or closure; the police/agencies have power over the offender (e.g. to punish) but public opinion shapes how this is done; the victim and the offender can appeal to the public (e.g. by appearing in the news media or just talking to friends and family).

In normal retributive justice, the police/agencies punish the offender, perhaps encouraged by public opinion, and the victim is side-lined. In RJ, the victim is put back into the equation and gets a say in how things are resolved.

John Braithwaite (1989) argues that retributive punishment causes **disintegrative shaming** – a sense of worthlessness that leads to reoffending. RJ leads to **integrative shaming**, which enables the offender to move on and re-join society. This is the opposite of the Right Wing view of **retribution leading to moral self-knowledge** (p139) and it assumes that offenders are genuine in their restorations (and not just saying what the victims and authorities expect of them).

AO2 ILLUSTRATION: FORGIVENESS FOR AMBER GUYGER

In 2018, off-duty (White) Dallas police office **Amber Guyger** shot and killed (Black) **Botham Jean**, believing he was an intruder (in fact she had walked into his apartment by mistake). She was convicted of murder. During the trial, **Brandt Jean**, the brother of the victim, announced he forgave Guyger and hugged her, asking her to *"give your life to Christ."* The gesture was widely watched on TV.

This isn't an example of RJ, because it was a gesture in court inspired by Brandt Jean's Christian faith, rather than a planned meeting between the offender and the victim's family. However, Brandt Jean's mother said, *"Your load is lighter"* afterwards, which is the desired outcome for RJ.

There were criticisms of the gesture, with one online commentator posting: *"America should ask Black people forgiveness for serially asking African Americans to forgive sanctioned #PoliceBrutality."* This illustrates a problem that RJ, by making the crime a private matter between victim and offender, can remove the need for **structural change in society** (p147).

Research: research real cases of RJ; watch the 2016 ITV documentary *Meeting My Enemy* about Jacob Dunne

RESEARCH PROFILE: SHERMAN & STRANG (2007)

Lawrence Sherman & Heather Strang carried out a review of good practice in RJ to determine its effectiveness. They gathered 424 research studies from an Internet search and reduced this to 34 studies from the UK, USA and Australia that provided an experimental comparison of a group experiencing RJ and a control group going through ordinary justice procedures.

The RJ groups showed a reduction in offending for violent and property offences; the victims showed reduced trauma and desire for revenge; they reported an increased ability to come to terms with what had happened. The researchers recommend RJ is more widely used in the UK.

The studies all involve small sample groups and come from different countries with different legal systems, making it hard to generalise the findings to the UK in all cases.

STRUCTURAL CHANGE IN SOCIETY

People who support Left Wing policies demand a structural change in society – not just tinkering with particular situations but changing the way society works for everyone. Left Wing criminology often focuses on the use of benefits to lift families out of poverty, reform of the police to change the way they interact with communities and challenging **institutional racism** in all areas of life.

Research: review your notes on **Section A** and focus on Social Justice (p53) and the Anti-Globalisation Movement (p13) as examples of campaigning for structural change

Many Left Wing ideas are inspired by **Merton**'s insight that crime is caused by **structural strain** in society (p120). By reducing the strain (making society more equal), you reduce incentives for crime.

*Wait, isn't Merton a **Functionalist**? Yes, but **Strain Theory** influenced **Neo-Marxism** and **Left Realism**, who abandoned the Functionalist stuff about anomie but kept the focus on inequality*

For example, former chief constable Andy Cooke told **The Guardian** that if he had £5 billion to cut crime, he would put £1 billion into policing and £4 billion into reducing poverty: "*The best crime prevention is increased opportunity and reduced poverty*" (source: **Vikram Dodd, 2021**).

The **2018 Global Law & Order Report** suggests there is a correlation between equality and crime. 148,000 people in 142 countries completed a **victim survey** (p89) on whether they feel safe walking home alone and whether they trust the police. Countries were ranked according to how equally wealth is distributed there. In Venezuela, 80% do not feel safe walking home alone—kidnappings are common and it is the 19th most unequal in wealth. In Norway, 93% feel safe, but it is the 12th most equal country of the 142.

However, a correlation cannot prove cause-and-effect – and the country that comes out on top for safety is Singapore (94%) but Singapore is nowhere near the top for equality of wealth, so there must be other factors too.

A criticism of structural change is that it can just as easily **create** crime, since the outcomes are unpredictable. **Durkheim** (p77) argues that periods of rapid social change create **anomie**, even if those changes involve increasing equality.

For example, in 2001 the UK Labour government introduced **Working Family Tax Credits (WFTC)** to support low-paid families with children. The scheme was very popular and helped alleviate 'in-work poverty' and make working worthwhile (so it also addressed the New Right's criticism of benefit traps creating an **Underclass**, p122). However, it was blamed for driving up divorce, because a single mother could claim an extra £100 per week by splitting from her partner; in the three years after WFTC was introduced, the divorce rate among women with low-income husbands rose 160% (source: **Francesconi et al, 2009**). Right Wing critics argue that divorce contributes to delinquency and men without family responsibilities are more likely to be deviant.

*Robert Merton termed this the 'law of unintended consequences' – when you interfere with a complex system, you cannot predict all the outcomes. It is often used by Right Wingers (e.g. **James Q Wilson**, p124) to justify sticking with the status quo because any change might be for the worse.*

146

AO2 ILLUSTRATION: CAPITAL HILL AUTONOMOUS ZONE (Chaz)

In 2020, the murder of a Black American named **George Floyd** by a police officer sparked worldwide protests under the banner of the **Black Lives Matter** movement (p79). Protestors in the Capital Hill area of Seattle formed an 'autonomous zone' (Chaz) where they banned the police from entering. They distributed free food and medical supplies and planted community gardens. One small group painted a large mural: *Black Lives Matter*.

Seattle's mayor Jenny Durkan said the zone could be the start of a "*summer of love.*" A visitor to Chaz described it to the BBC: "*There were classes, lectures, speakers, poetry, lots of live music, huge works of art... It was really beautiful.*"

The Chaz protestors demanded that funding for the police be cut by half and the money re-directed to health care and **restorative justice** (p145).

There were four shootings within the zone, two of which were fatal; allegations of sexual assaults emerged. Chaz supporters denied that these were carried out by the protesters. Nevertheless, on 1 July 2020, after 3 weeks of occupation, the police used force to clear the site (and reclaim their police station), with Seattle police chief Carmen Best declaring, "*Enough is enough.*"

If you are Left Wing, then Chaz indicates the possibility of a police-free society, which would be a huge structural change. If you are Right Wing, it illustrates the impossibility of such a utopia.

Welcome to Chaz (photo: Derek Simeone)

Research: find out more about Chaz and the other autonomous zones created by protestors in 2020; review your notes on **1A: Socialisation, Culture & Identity** and link this to **Defunding The Police** and **formal agencies of social control**

RESEARCH PROFILE: SULLIVAN & O'KEEFFE (2017)

In 2014 in New York, **Eric Garner** was killed while being arrested, triggering protests that ended with two police officers being fatally shot by an anti-police extremist. In response, New York Police Department (NYPD) conducted a **slowdown** for 7 weeks: they performed only essential duties and stopped issuing traffic tickets and using Stop & Search powers.

Christopher Sullivan & Zachary O'Keeffe analysed the **official crime statistics** during the slowdown. The arrest rate for serious crime (murder, rape, robbery, etc.) remained constant because these were still being policed normally. Minor crimes and drug offences dropped by 3-6%. This could be because the public didn't bother reporting crimes but the researchers identify the drop in crime lasting for a period after the slowdown finished. They suggest instead it was the ***absence of police*** that led to the reduction in crime.

The researchers suggest that the slowdown was *"a symbolic show of strength to demonstrate the city's dependence on the NYPD"* – but it seems to have demonstrated the opposite.

Sullivan & O'Keeffe conclude that proactive policing (when the police are on the streets looking for law-breaking to happen) actually ***disrupts*** communities and makes crimes more likely. This is a powerful argument against **Zero Tolerance Policing** (p140) and in favour of defunding the police.

However, it is based on an unusual period in New York City following a crisis of confidence in the NYPD and the results might not generalise to other cities and times. For example, in 2020 over 20 US cities (including New York) cut police budgets by a total of $840 million; however, the murder rate went up by 25% that year and America experienced a surge in violence. Critics debate whether this increase is due to reduced policing, the stresses of the 2020-22 Coronavirus Pandemic or other factors (like the possible end of the **Great Crime Decline**, p95).

New York Police (photo: Matthias Kinsella)

Evaluating Left Wing Views on Crime Reduction

Left Wing views on crime reduction are less popular with the general public but have had more influence on social policy in the last 20 years.

Social and **community crime prevention** have been used by many governments and might explain much of the **Great Crime Decline** (p95). However, these policies are expensive. They are defended on the grounds that the money spent on them produces greater savings later (when future-criminals get jobs and pay taxes instead of going to prison and costing tax money). The law of unintended consequences means that these outcomes are never certain: training future-criminals in problem-solving might just make them more effective criminals, after all.

This sort of crime prevention and control also raises concerns, especially the role of Big Government in ordinary people's lives. Right Wingers claim that government meddling always backfires and regard the family as under threat (e.g. the controversy over the impact of Working Family Tax Credits).

The most interesting aspect of Left Wing criminology is **Restorative Justice (RJ)**. This promises to be a new approach and one which is compatible with defunding the police and putting fewer people in prison. It also offers closure for victims who are often ignored (the Right Wing alternative, **retributive justice**, only reassures victims that the offender is suffering horribly). However, RJ only works if all parties volunteer for it and there are some crimes (e.g. rape) where being confronted by your abuser might *increase*, rather than reduce, the victim's trauma. It's possible to fake guilt and repentance and offenders who are **psychopaths** excel at this sort of deception and manipulation.

Moreover, reconciling victim and offender does nothing to fix structural problems in society and might even make them worse – such as insisting that Black victims of crime or police brutality ought to forgive their attacker rather than White people fixing the **institutional racism** in society. Of course, it's possible to do both and the **Square of Crime** reminds us that the public and the police/agencies are involved in every crime too.

Focusing on **structural changes in society** offers the hope of dealing with crime at the source: the inequality in society. The main criticism of this is that, by blaming society for crime and misbehaviour, Left Wingers neglect the offender's individual and personal responsibility. Crime is no longer seen as a moral problem that needs to be judged and condemned, but an economic or medical problem that needs to be cured.

On the other hand, Left Wing approaches do focus on the idea that crime is a **social construct** (p83) and that no one would choose to be a criminal and go to prison if they had better alternatives available to them. The job of Left Wing policies is to offer people those better choices. This often means challenging the assumption that we need heavy-handed policing or that there's nothing that can be done about poverty – or that it's a person's own fault that they are poor. Left Wing policies often claim to be motivated by compassion for the vulnerable people in society and that sometimes means compassion for criminals too.

EXAM PRACTICE: REDUCING CRIME & DEVIANCE

The OCR exam has three questions in **Paper 3 Section B**. Questions 7-9 are on Education and questions 10-12 are on Religion, Belief & Faith, but this Study Guide is focused on **Option 1** which covers questions **4-6**:

4. In what ways do crime prevention strategies reduce crime? **[10 marks: 6 AO1 + 4 AO2]**

This is one of those 'describe & illustrate' questions, but with no Source A or Source B to lean on. No need to evaluate.

*Choose two strategies to outline – you could choose Left Wing ones or Right Wing ones or one of each. It's a good idea to refer to named sociologists (like Clarke or Parks) and you should definitely use some sociological terminology (like structural inequality, rational choice). Then offer examples and make sure each example has an explanation of **why** it prevents crime. For example, "Target hardening includes steering locks on cars which makes it not worth the trouble for a rational criminal to break into a car."*

5. To what extent is restorative justice an effective strategy for reducing crime? **[20 marks: 8 AO1 + 4 AO2 + 8 AO3]**

This is a mid-size essay with a requirement for developed evaluation. You should spend 25 minutes and write at least 500 words.

*Write **three** points. Each point should introduce a sociological idea with some illustration from the real world. Each should finish off with a developed evaluation. For example, you could write about Zehr's three pillars, the Square of Crime and integrative shaming. Don't forget to offer a conclusion: will RJ actually work (Sherman & Strang is important for this)?*

6. Outline and evaluate Right Wing policies for reducing crime and deviance. **[40 marks: 16 AO1 + 8 AO2 + 16 AO3]**

This is the last of the two big (40 mark) essays in OCR A-Level Sociology. You should spend 50 minutes and write at least 1000 words.

*Write **five** points. Each point should introduce a sociological idea with illustration from the real world. Each should finish off with a developed evaluation. For example, you could write about target hardening, architectural policies, custodial sentences, the death penalty and Zero Tolerance Policing. The differing views of Functionalists, Right Realists and Marxists could all come into this as well as the question about whether Right Wing policies actually work (defunding the police is a useful issue to answer this).*

CHAPTER 9 – EVALUATION

In **Paper 3 Section B (Option 1: Crime & Deviance)**, question 5 and 6 both assess **AO3**/evaluation and require a developed evaluation; this needs to address theoretical or methodological issues. It needs to go deeper than a 'brief evaluation' and look at an issue from alternative perspectives or work through the implications of a viewpoint.

As well as the evaluative points you can find in the preceding chapters, here are some evaluative positions candidates can adopt:

Brief Evaluations

These points are simple one that are hard to turn into developed points, so you might miss out on the higher AO3 band marks. Still, better to write something than nothing at all.

"Not all people…" / Over-generalising

Structuralist Perspectives (like **Functionalism** or traditional **Marxism** and **Feminism**) are particularly prone to sweeping generalisations. They often claim that everyone is motivated by the same thing or experiences the same oppression or wants the same outcomes. For example, Functionalists claim everyone shares the same basic values in society and Feminists claim all women are in some way oppressed.

To evaluate these ideas, point out that not all people fit into this mould. Not all unemployed people commit crimes, not all police are racist, not all criminals are deterred by the death penalty.

If you are writing about some empirical research, point out that its sample group doesn't resemble everyone. Not all delinquents are white like the ones that William Chambliss studied (p132).

It's important not to be formulaic. Say *why* not all people are like this: give an example of one of the exceptions. Not all criminals are deterred by the death penalty, because some people commit crimes *under the influence of drugs*. Not all delinquent teenagers are like Chambliss' schoolboys *because some are Black or Asian and they have their own problems with racism*.

"It's out-of-date…" / Time-locked

You will probably have noticed that an awful lot of sociological research comes from the 1950s, '60s and '70s. Those were important decades when a lot of ground-breaking Sociology was done. But do theories and samples from the 1970s tell us anything about the UK in the 21st century?

To evaluate these studies, point out that so much has changed. **Mass employment in factories has ended, equal rights for women** has arrived (at least, in principle), the UK has **become a multicultural socie**ty, the **Internet** has transformed the way we communicate and find out about the world (this last point makes studies from the 1980s and early '90s out-of-date too).

Once again, it's important not to be formulaic. Say *why* one of these changes matters for this particular study: give an example of one of the exceptions. Holdaway's study of police occupational culture (p88) is out of date because *the Metropolitan Police has reformed itself after the Macpherson Report*. Chambliss' research into the Saints & Roughnecks (p132) is out-of-date *because in the 21ˢᵗ century, schools and towns have CCTV to catch kids truanting or misbehaving*.

"Nature rather than nurture..." / The Nature-Nurture Debate

Sociologists tend to assume that everything is socially constructed, but it's worth remembering that biology might be playing a neglected role in human behaviour.

To evaluate these ideas, point out that a Nativist approach might be better. Rather than explain crime through social control, maybe there are innate biological processes that go on in criminals.

It would be formulaic just to say "maybe there are innate biological changes" and leave it at that. Say *why* the Nativist approach would be better: give an example of one of the benefits. Take a Nativist approach to studying crime, *because it might tell you the role testosterone places in male crime in lots of different cultures*.

Developing Evaluations

These points are suitable for Q5 or Q6. Their complexity makes them suitable for turning into developed points, so you can qualify for higher AO3 band marks.

"It's a macro-perspective / Interactionist critique

Structuralist Perspectives make sweeping generalisations because they study society as a whole and focus on important institutions rather than individual people. The **Interactionist** Perspective criticises this, saying it is better to look at society 'from the bottom up' (a **micro Perspective**). The sociologist Max Weber recommends using *Verstehen* – empathic understanding – rather than focusing on big trends.

To evaluate these ideas, point out that an Interactionist approach might be better. Rather than studying the Underclass as a trend in society, take a micro approach and study individual members of the Underclass.

Avoid being formulaic. Say *why* the micro approach would be better: give an example of one of the benefits. Take a micro approach to studying the Underclass, *because they will tell you why they are unemployed, which may or may not have anything to do with a benefits trap*.

Development

If you bring in Interactionism as the solution to the problem, don't stop there. You could give examples of studies that employ this micro approach (like **Chambliss** studying delinquents, p132) or explain how later research incorporates aspects of the micro approach (like the way Left Realism involves the **Square of Crime**, p145).

Alternatively, criticise your own improvement: discuss the drawbacks of using the micro approach (the Underclass people might lie to the interviewer; after all, they are supposed to have no sense of right and wrong according to **Murray**, p123).

"This is similar to..." / Comparisons

Sometimes, different sociologists or different Perspectives end up saying similar things, although usually for different reasons Marxists and Feminists both agree there is propaganda and brainwashing (**ideology**) in the news. Marxists and Functionalists both agree that modern Capitalism is stressful and difficult for the poor. Interactionists and Marxists both agree that the police label people.

To evaluate these ideas, point out the similarity between the sociology you are writing about and another Perspective or research study. If you have explained that Marxists think that there is selective policing, explain that Interactionists also think that labels create a moral panic about 'folk devils' (p101).

As usual, don't be formulaic. Say *why* the two approaches are so similar *or* say why they are also different: give an example. Marxists and Interactionist agree on policing because they both think that crime is socially constructed, *although Marxists think this comes from serving the ruling class* and *Interactionists focus more on how moral panics lead to deviancy amplification spirals*.

Development

If you think two Perspectives are similar, don't stop there. You could give examples of studies from each perspective, like **Hall**'s study of moral panics about Black muggers (p99) compared to **Cohen**'s study of Mods & Rockers (p101); or explain how later research incorporates both perspectives, like the Neo-Marxists of *The New Criminology* using Interactionist techniques.

Alternatively, criticise the very similarity you suggested: discuss the how differences between the two approaches are more important than similarities (Marxists recognise the overall social context of Capitalism, whereas Interactionists look at each social situation separately and miss out on the big picture).

"A Left/Right Winger would say …" / Political critique

Research into crime and deviance has a practical application: politicians use these ideas to pass laws and to launch or abolish social policies. Some of these are successful, others backfire. It's a good idea to praise sociological research if it leads to effective social policies or criticise it if it doesn't.

In order to avoid being formulaic, say *why* the research has practical benefits or drawbacks: give an example. Victim surveys support Left Wing approaches to crime prevention, *because they give the victim's perspective, which is important for Restorative Justice.*

Development

If you think a political implication is good or bad, don't stop there. You could give examples of studies which back up this political position, such as **Sherman & Strang**'s recommendations that RJ is widely used in the UK (p146).

Alternatively, criticise the political idea you suggested: discuss the flaws with focusing too much on victims (such as the way it can distract Left Wingers from working towards **structural change in society**).

"A weakness of this Perspective is …" / Standard theoretical critiques

Functionalism

Functionalism ignores diversity: Functionalism assumes we are all the same and want the same things, but the things it says we all want tend to be the sort of things that the white middle classes want. Functionalism doesn't take seriously the idea that ethnic minorities, the working class or women might have different goals and values.

Functionalism ignores social injustice: Functionalism assumes that society is harmonious and **meritocratic** but it turns a blind eye to a lot of inequality, corruption and barriers to social mobility. It defends Capitalism as the best system we have discovered for making people healthy and wealthy while ignoring the huge human and environmental cost of Capitalism worldwide. It is also prepared to accept a lot of crime for the sake of consensus.

Functionalism celebrates Western superiority: Functionalists believe in the **'March of Progress'** and claim that the sort of liberal democratic nations you find in Europe, North America and Australia are the most advanced. Other societies ought to imitate them and immigrants ought to fit in. This ignores many flaws in Western societies (e.g. Capitalism, patriarchy, institutional racism).

Functionalism overrates the biological: Functionalists believe society reflects unchangeable biological needs or 'human nature.' Critics argue there is no such thing as 'human nature' and that everything is **socially constructed**. 'Human nature' is often used to excuse certain crimes (such as male violence, prostitution or rape).

Development

If you offer a theoretical weakness, don't stop there. You could give examples of studies that illustrate that weakness (like Falk's study that suggests a small number of people commit most of the serious crime). Alternatively, follow through the implications of this weakness (what would happen if Right Wing politicians acted on Functionalist ideas) or bring in other Perspectives that have something to say about this weakness (like Marxists characterising Functionalist ideas as serving hegemonic power).

Alternatively, criticise the weakness you suggested by arguing that it isn't really a weakness: like James Q Wilson's idea that the factors involved in making a more equal society are beyond anyone's control so it's better to focus on what can be controlled and change the physical environment to reduce crime.

Make a point of discussing how Subcultural Theory improves on the standard Functionalist position in various ways – but at the cost of abandoning certain important Functionalist ideas. You can discuss how Right Realism improves on Functionalism in the same way.

The New Right

The New Right lacks empirical support: Most of the support for the New Right comes from news stories about working class deviance – but those stories might be exaggerated. Hard evidence for the existence of an **underclass** is not plentiful and there's even less evidence for a whole group of people (rather than a few individuals) who reject society's values, don't want to work, don't want to live in families and embrace crime as a lifestyle.

The New Right demonises the vulnerable: The New Right is accused of 'punching down' – targeting the group in society that most needs help and making them out to be monstrous and calling for any sort of help (in the form of benefits) to be taken away. **Marxists** find it fairly easy to characterise the New Right as a **hegemonic attack on the poor**. However, Marxists can be characterised as glamorising delinquents and criminals as noble underdogs and ignoring the damage they do in society.

The New Right exaggerates deviancy: The New Right presents the underclass as a growing problem that threatens the whole of society. Even **Functionalists** criticise this approach as alarmist. Functionalists believe that deviancy is necessary and ultimately benefits society. However, the New Right emerged partly because both Functionalists and Marxists seemed to be making excuses for crime rather than doing anything practical to put a stop to it.

Development

If you offer a theoretical weakness, don't stop there. You could give examples of studies that illustrate that weakness (like Murray's warning that single mothers are raising feral boys and promiscuous girls illustrates the New Right demonising the vulnerable). Alternatively, follow through the implications of this weakness (what would happen if politicians acted on Murray's suggestions) or bring in other Perspectives that have something to say about this weakness (like Marxists characterising the attack as serving hegemonic power).

Alternatively, criticise the weakness you suggested by arguing that it isn't really a weakness: Murray thinks the real enemies of the poor are the people who keep them in a benefits trap that appears kind but is actually dehumanising – you would be doing the underclass a favour by getting them off benefits and into family arrangements.

Make a point of discussing how Right Realism improves on the standard New Right position in various ways – but at the cost of abandoning certain important New Right ideas.

Marxism

Marxism ignores progress: In the last 200 years, Capitalist societies have abolished slavery, set up human rights, created a welfare state and free education and healthcare for all. Marxists often talk as if this hasn't happened or as if it happened *in spite of* Capitalism. This pessimistic view of the past and the future perhaps exaggerates social injustice as much as Functionalism downplays it.

Marxism is a conspiracy theory: It's standard for Marxists to argue that the Media (especially the news), Education and the Workplace are all controlled by a sinister group of billionaires who brainwash everyone through **ideology**. This underestimates the independence of many journalists, politicians and police officers well as the ability of ordinary people to think for themselves and work out what's true.

Marxists assume class is homogenous: *Homogenous* means 'all the same' and traditional Marxists think that all working class people share the same relationship to labour and power. However, **Neo-Marxists** are more aware of **intersecting Identities** and how behaviour is shaped by the particular circumstances.

Marxism offers no solutions: You don't have to be a Marxist to spot the Capitalism has flaws – Functionalists would admit *that*! Marxists argue that Capitalism is intrinsically rotten and destructive and it needs to be replaced rather than reformed. But replaced with what? Marxism can be accused of criticising Capitalism without offering a coherent alternative. Similarly, it identifies Youth Deviance as resistance, but doesn't suggest what can be done about its destructive aspects.

Development

If you offer a theoretical weakness, develop them. You could give examples of studies that illustrate that weakness (like Sullivan & O'Keeffe suggesting the police could be defunded without saying what should be put in its place). Alternatively, follow through the implications of this weakness (what would happen if Left Wing politicians acted on Marxist suggestions) or bring in other Perspectives that have something to say about this weakness (like Functionalists characterising Marxism as ignoring the impact of crimes on victims).

Alternatively, criticise the weakness you suggested by arguing that it isn't really a weakness: Marxism might sometimes look like a conspiracy theory but the big newspapers, Right Wing politicians and police chiefs could all be 'on the same side' without deliberately conspiring so long as they share vested interests.

Make a point of discussing how Neo-Marxism improves on the standard Marxist position in various ways – but at the cost of abandoning certain important Marxist ideas. You can discuss how Left Realism improves on Neo-Marxism in the same way.

Feminism

Feminism ignores biology: Feminists insist that gender is **socially constructed,** and it certainly is up to a point. However, Psychology reveals lots of biological differences in brain structure, hormones and genes between the sexes and it's unlikely that *none* of this makes *any* difference to social behaviour. But if Gender Identity is even partly based on unchangeable sexual differences, then some of the situations women are in might not be *entirely* due to Patriarchy.

Feminism ignores progress: In the last century women have won the vote, the right to be educated at university and manage their own affairs. In Britain, the Sexual Discrimination Act (1975) has outlawed sexual discrimination. Feminism can be accused of downplaying this progress and exaggerating the scale of injustice. However, the Sarah Everard murder can be used to show that women in the 21st century are still not safe.

Feminists assume gender is homogenous: As with Marxists and social class, traditional Feminists are accused of treating all women as if they experienced the same oppression – which in practice means assuming that the difficulties of White women are typical for all women. Clearly, young women (and especially young lesbian women) have different experiences.

Feminists ignore the oppression of men: Feminists sometimes seem to assume that Masculinity is homogenous and all men are complicit in the Patriarchy, but men are much more likely than women to die by violence, to be victims of crime and to work in dangerous conditions. Many young men are also victims of oppression and die in dangerous jobs, through violence or suicide.

Development

If you offer a theoretical weakness, develop it. You could give examples of studies that illustrate that weakness (like Adler arguing that progress in women's liberation has encouraged female crime while ignoring testosterone in male crime). Alternatively, follow through the implications of this weakness (what would happen if Left Wing politicians acted on Feminist suggestions, such as the 'curfew on men') or bring in other Perspectives that have something to say about this weakness (like Marxists agreeing that Capitalism oppresses men and women in different ways).

Alternatively, criticise the weakness you suggested by arguing that it isn't really a weakness: Feminism might ignore progress but the murder of Sarah Everard shows that women are still being murdered by men and the police who are supposed to protect them do not do so.

You could discuss how 4th Wave Feminism improves on the standard Feminist position in various ways – but at the cost of abandoning certain important Feminist ideas.

Interactionism

Interactionism cannot be generalised: Because it tends to do research on small groups, studying micro relationships and beliefs, it's hard to generalise the conclusions of Interactionism to other groups or society on a macro level.

Interactionists cannot be objective: The close-up and personal nature of Interactionist research and its focus on **Verstehen** makes it very **subjective** – just a matter of opinion – whereas Sociology claims to be a social *science* that explores facts in an **objective** way.

Interactionism is an incomplete explanation: Even when Interaction identifies processes that seem to be quite generalisable – like the **Self-Fulfilling Prophecy** – its small-scale micro view means it doesn't explore where these processes come from. Marxists argue that Interactionism is incomplete as an explanation without including Capitalism and **ruling class ideology**. Functionalists would also say Interactionism needs to explain how the experiences of little groups fit into a theory of society's functions and requirements.

Development

If you offer a theoretical weakness, develop them. You could give examples of studies that illustrate that weakness (like Chambliss' study being limited to Seattle teenagers or Cohen to the 1960s). Alternatively, follow through the implications of this weakness (what would happen if politicians acted on Interactionist suggestions) or bring in other Perspectives that have something to say about this weakness (like Neo-Marxism claiming to offer an explanation of where labels come from in the first place).

Alternatively, criticise the weakness you suggested by arguing that it isn't really a weakness: Interactionism might lack objectivity but the point about *verstehen* is that it gives insight into what 'makes people tick' rather than focusing on statistics or mass trends.

You could discuss how Neo-Marxism and Left Realism improve on the standard Interactionist position in various ways – but perhaps at the cost of abandoning the micro perspective in Interactionism.

EXAM PRACTICE: SECTION B

The OCR exam has three questions in **Paper 3 Section B**. Questions 7-9 are on Education and questions 10-12 are on Religion, Belief & Faith, but this Study Guide is focused on **Option 1** which covers questions **4-6**:

4. In what ways is victimisation distributed differently by age? **[10 marks: 6 AO1 + 4 AO2]**

This is one of those 'describe & illustrate' questions, but with no Source A or Source B to lean on. No need to evaluate.

*Choose two points to outline – you could choose the young and the elderly. It's a good idea to refer to named sociologists (like Farrington) and you should definitely use some sociological terminology (like life course, fear of crime vs vulnerability to crime). Then offer examples and make sure each example has an explanation of **why** it involves victimisation of an age group. For example, "Elderly people are less at risk of crime because they don't go out to unfamiliar or dangerous places as much as the young but 8 out of 10 doorstep scams are carried out on the elderly."*

5. To what extent is the New Right an effective explanation for crime and deviance? **[20 marks: 8 AO1 + 4 AO2 + 8 AO3]**

This is a mid-size essay with a requirement for developed evaluation. You should spend 25 minutes and write at least 500 words.

*Write **three** points. Each point should introduce a sociological idea with some illustration from the real world. Each should finish off with a developed evaluation. For example, you could write about worklessness, illegitimate births and Murray's idea of the benefits trap. Don't forget to offer a conclusion: does the New Right actually explain anything?*

6. Outline and evaluate Left Wing policies for reducing crime and deviance. **[40 marks: 16 AO1 + 8 AO2 + 16 AO3]**

This is the last of the two big (40 mark) essays in OCR A-Level Sociology. You should spend 50 minutes and write at least 1000 words.

*Write **four** points. Each point should introduce a sociological idea with illustration from the real world. Each should finish off with a developed evaluation. For example, you could write about social crime prevention, community service, restorative justice, reducing inequality and defunding the police. The differing views of Marxists, Neo-Marxists and Left Realists could all come into this as well as the question about whether Left Wing policies actually work (examples like Chaz and WFTC could help with this).*

KEY RESEARCH

The 31 studies here cover all the topics that arise in this Section of the exam and they will prove just as useful in later sections too. Start learning them. For each study, I include the key terms, a Perspective (if relevant) and the particular topics it is linked to.

Adler (1975): *Sisters In Crime*, Liberation Thesis, female criminality; **Feminist**; social construction, relativism, patterns of gender, p105

Bates (2014): *Everyday Sexism*, **Feminist**; social construction, relativism, patterns of gender, p100

Beck (1992): *The Risk Society*, late modernity, risk, transgressive criminology; **Interactionist**; green crime, p114

Beckett & Evans (2018): capital punishment, implicit bias; **Left Realist**; social construction, relativism, patterns of ethnicity, retributive justice, p140

Chambliss (1973): *The Saints & the Roughnecks*, labelling; **Interactionist, Neo-Marxist**; Interactionist/Neo-Marxist explanations, p132

Cloward & Ohlin (1960): legitimate & illegitimate opportunity structures, criminal, conflict, retreatist; **Functionalist**; Subcultural explanation, p121

Cohen, S (1972): *Folk Devils & Moral Panics*, 1964 Mods v Rockers riots; **Interactionism**; media & deviance, p101

Falk et al. (2013): Swedish study, chronic offenders; **Functionalist**; patterns & trends, p98

Farrington et al. (2006): *Cambridge Study*, longitudinal, chronic offenders; **Interactionist**; self-report study, patterns of age, p110

Fitzgerald et al. (2002): *Policing For London*, institutional racism; **Left Realist**; social construction, relativism, patterns of ethnicity, p107

Glenny (2008): *McMafia*, McDonalisation of crime, Bulgarian Mafia; organised global crime, p112

Gordon (1971): *Class & the Economics of Crime*, selective policing; **Neo-Marxist**; Marxist explanations, p126

Hall (1978): *Policing the Crisis*, moral panic over Black muggers; **Neo-Marxist**; subculture & ethnicity, deviant delinquent subcultures, media & deviance, p99

Holdaway (1980): police occupational culture, police discretion, selective policing; **Neo-Marxist**; patterns of class, social construction, p88

Jones (2011): *Chavs*, stigma, moral panic; **Neo-Marxist**; social construction, relativism, patterns of class, p103

Jones, Maclean & Young (1986): Islington Crime Survey; **New Right**; patterns of class & gender, victim survey, p90

Lea & Young (1984): *What's To Be Done About Law & Order?*, relative deprivation, marginalisation, subculture; **Left Realist**; Left Realist explanations, p128

Merton (1938): Strain Theory, anomie, innovation; **Functionalism**; Functionalist explanation, p120

Mumsnet (2012): Sexual Assault Survey; **Feminist**; victim survey, patterns of gender, p86

Murray (1984): underclass; **New Right**; New Right explanation, patterns of class, p123

Newman (1972): *Defensible Space*, architecture; **Functionalist**; environmental crime prevention, p138

Parks (1988): Perry Preschool Project; **Left Realist**; community crime prevention, patterns of age, p144

Pearson (1983): *Hooligans*, Teddy boys; **Neo-Marxist**; social construction, relativism, patterns of age, p85

Punch (2007): Zero Tolerance Policing; **Right Realist**; punitive control, p141

Sharkey (2018): *Uneasy Peace*, Great Crime Decline; **Left Realist**; patterns & trends, social policies, p97

Shaw (1930): *The Jack Roller*; **Interactionist**; self-report studies, patterns of age, p93

Sherman & Strang (2007): restorative justice; **Left Realist**; restorative justice, p146

Smart (1976): *Women, Crime & Criminology*, strict socialisation, doubly deviant; **Feminist**; Feminist explanations, patterns of gender, p131

Sullivan & O'Keeffe (2017): NYPD slowdown, Zero Tolerance Policing; **Left Realist**; structural change, punitive control, p148

Taylor, Walton & Young (1972): *The New Criminology*, critical criminology, fully social theory; **Neo-Marxist**; Radical Criminology explanations, p127

Wilson (1975): *Thinking About Crime*, social order, rational choice; **Neo-Marxist**; Right Realist explanations, p124

FURTHER RESEARCH

These studies are less central to any argument. Some of them just reference a useful piece of terminology. Others offer criticism of a Key Study or are the original research that a Key Study is criticising.

Alexander (1997): sex work is liberating, p105

Becker (1963): *Outsiders*, labelling theory, p84

Bindel (2017): sex work is rape, p130

Bourgois (1995): relative deprivation, p94

Box (1983): selective policing, p92

Braithwaite (1989): supports restorative justice, p146

Campbell (1981): self-reports show no gender divide, p92

Clarke (1983): crime prevention, p137

Cohen (1955): status frustration, p121

Cornish & Clarke (1986): rational choice theory, p123

Durkheim (1883): social solidarity, p77

Durkheim (1895): society of saints, p83

Estrada et al. (20015): male crime patterns resembling women's, p105

Farrell (2007): CSEW underestimates crime, p90

Francesconi et al. (2009): criticises WFTC, p147

Garfinkel (1956): criticises retributive justice, p139

Heidensohn (1985): criticises Chivalry Thesis, p130

Hobbs & Dunningham (1998): glocalised organised crime, p111

Hollin (1989): Dark Figure of unrecorded crime, p86

Lambert (1970): police discretion, p88

Lemert (1967): secondary deviance, p131

Hanley (2011): criticises **Jones (2011)**, p103

Jackson (2006): 'laddish' girls, p105

Marx (1858): base and superstructure, p77

Matthews & Young (1992): the Square of Crime, p145

Parsons (1951): functional prerequisites valve, p80

Pearson & Rowe (2020): bias in Stop & Search, p106

Phillips (1999): criticises **Murray (1984)**, p123

South (2008): primary vs secondary green crime, p112

Snodgrass (1972): followed up **Shaw (1930)**, p93

Thompson et al. (2012): crime peaks in 2003, p96

Valenti (2011): supports SlutWalks, p85

Walklate (1995): criticises Chivalry Thesis, p130

Weber (1905): invention of Capitalism, p81

Weber (1922): social actions, p78

White (2008): anthropocentric vs ecocentric harm, p113

Young (1984): social bulimia, p125

Young (2003): criticises New Right, p122

Zehr (2003): *Changing Lenses*, restorative justice, p145

GLOSSARY

Anomie: literally means "without norms" and it refers to the sense of disconnection and anxiety that occurs when people do not feel a connection to their society and their work; Functionalists say it is caused by the breakdown of **social solidity** and a lack of **value consensus**

Capitalism: an economic system that promotes the private ownership of property, the pursuit of profit and the concentration of wealth in the hands of a minority of people; the opposite is Communism, which abolishes private property to make everyone economically equal

Crime: an act that breaks the laws of the state, bringing formal sanctions on the criminal

Cultural defence: ways that members of a culture can resist **homogenisation** due to **globalisation**; may lead to **glocalisation**

Culture: the set of norms and values passed on by one generation to the next, including a version of history and traditional institutions that make up a way of life; cultures vary from one society to another and change (slowly) over time

Deconstruction: technique to expose the hidden values in **discourse** and weaken the power encoded in language, usually by exposing bias, questioning ordinary meanings and playing around with possible meanings.

Deterrence: the effect of making people law-abiding by showing them the negative consequences of crime for themselves

Deviance: Behaviour that goes against **norms** and **values**

Deviancy Amplification Spiral: a process where a deviant **label** is acted upon by the authorities, leading to harsh sanctions and increased attention paid to the **deviancy**, exaggerating the **moral panic**

Digital Divide: the separation of people into those who can and those who cannot take full advantage of the Internet

Digital Forms of Communication (DFOC): ways of interacting with other people through the Internet, such as sending or receiving text messages or emails or posting on websites

Digital Revolution: transformation in communications technology brought on by the invention of computers

Discourse: a way of using language that is coded with assumptions about power and privilege; using this language reinforces inequality in society but **deconstructing** it can empower oppressed or marginalised groups

Feminism: a sociological Perspective that identified conflict between the sexes; believes in a Patriarchy which subordinates women and maintains male power through coercion and violence

Folk Devil: a group identified as a threat to society during a **moral panic**

Functionalism: a sociological Perspective that promotes consensus around shared values; believes in a biological basis for human social behaviour and the inevitability of deviance

Gender: the norms and values linked to biological sex; males are often expected to behave in a masculine way and females in a feminine way: male/female are sexes but masculine/feminine are genders

Globalisation: a process going on that makes different parts of the world more interconnected through travel, global **Capitalism** and the **Mass Media**; results in the spread of Global Culture and Hybrid Culture but is sometimes resisted

Glocalisation: a process combining the influence of **Globalisation** with local culture; may be a result of cultural defence creating a Hybrid Culture or a strategy by global Capitalism to make its products more attractive

Hegemony: the dominance of one group and their culture in society; hegemonic culture is the version of culture that commands the most respect; hegemonic culture might be the culture of the majority of people but it is more often the culture of a wealthy and influential elite

Heteronormative: privileging heterosexual people, stigmatising gays, lesbians and gender non-conformist or non-binary people

Homogenisation: a process of removing differences and distinctions so that everyone becomes similar; the opposite is heterogenisation

Ideology: a set of ideas and values that influence how people interpret society; ideology is usually promoted by the **hegemonic** culture hides and justifies things which go against that culture; for example, a racist ideology might make people ignore racism or (if they can't ignore it) view racism as justified

Institutional Racism: a form of systemic bias that makes people within an institution carry out racist practices even though they may not personally harbour racist views

Interactionism: a sociological Perspective that adopts a micro (small scale) approach; believes in understand individual motives and perceptions, often through examining how people play social roles or internalise **labels**

Intersectionality: A 21st century approach to Sociology which focuses on how different identities combine to create privilege or oppression

Labelling Theory: an **Interactionist** explanation of deviance due to social labels with master status that are internalised, producing a self-fulfilling prophecy, according to **Becker (1963)**

Latent function: The hidden effects of social institutions, that befit society without us noticing

Left Wing: a political tendency to value progress, equality and justice highly

Manifest function: The obvious effects of social institutions, that benefit society in ways we all recognise

Marxism: a sociological Perspective that identifies conflict between social classes; believes in a **ruling class** exploiting a **working class**, both through violet force and **ruling class ideology**

Mass Media: technological forms of communication that can reach millions (or billions of people); traditionally radio, TV, film and print but now including the digital media, such as websites, social media, text messaging and mobile phones

Materialism: traditional approach to **Marxism** and **2nd Wave Feminism** which focuses on identifying and challenging the inequality in people's material circumstances (as opposed to the language being used to describe them)

Meritocracy: A system that rewards talent and effort with social advancement; specifically, the idea that education recognises and gives qualifications to the most intelligent people, assigning them to the most important jobs with the biggest rewards. The opposite is **social reproduction**.

Moral Panic: process where the Media identifies a group as a threat, exaggerates its importance, arouses public concern and brings about new policies and social change

Multiculturalism: the idea that society can and should include people from different cultures without demanding that they abandon their native culture in order to assimilate

Neo-Marxism: several new interpretations of **Marxism** that emerged in the 1970s and became mainstream in the 1990s, incorporating elements of **Interactionism** to Marxist thought

New Media: platforms based around **digital forms of communication** that offer more interactivity and choice that the traditional media (e.g. satellite TV, streaming music or videos)

New Right: a sociological Perspective that proposes we are experiencing social collapse brought on by a welfare culture that rewards worklessness and deviance

Norms: ways of behaving seen as acceptable or expected in society; based on underlying **values**

Patriarchy: The way society is structured around the interests of males, giving status to masculine behaviour and values and systematically subordinating women; masculine **hegemony** in society

Post-Marxism: development of **Neo-Marxism** that incorporates **Postmodern** ideas about **discourse** and **deconstruction**

Postmodernism: a sociological Perspective that proposes we are living in a new phase of social development, characterised by media images, diversity, choice and fragmentation

Privilege: the advantages a person has, perhaps without realising it, because they belong to high-status groups or have Identities that are respected in society

Queer Theory: development of 3rd Wave Feminism that views society as dominated by **heteronormative discourses** that privilege straight men and which need to be 'queered' to show up their falseness

Right Wing: a political tendency to value privacy, freedom and family values highly

Ruling class: A **hegemonic** group in society that controls the wealth and power, supported by an ideology that either hides or justifies their influence; Marx termed the ruling class 'the bourgeoisie' but **Neo-Marxists** often term it the **Hegemony**

Ruling class ideology: a set of beliefs promoted by the ruling class to preserve their power over the working class; ideology hides the injustice in society and justifies it when it cannot hide it

Social capital: social connections (friends, family, followers, etc) which give you influence and power in society

Social class: A system for separating people based on their economic position (wealth, income, status); originally a split between the **ruling class** and **working class**, but later admitting of a middle class in between and now many more classes

Socialisation: The process of acquiring norms and values due to upbringing (primary socialisation) and education/experience (secondary socialisation)

Social reproduction: the opposite of **Meritocracy**; the idea that social divisions are reproduced each generation despite the education people receive

Social solidarity: The experience of 'belonging' in society, linked to **value consensus**; it is the opposite of **anomie**

Subculture: a group within society that shares some of the **norms and values** of mainstream society but also has distinctive norms and values of its own

Transgression: Behaviour that goes against the rules or laws; similar to **deviance**

Underclass: term used by the **New Right** for a class below the working class, characterised by single mothers on benefits, poorly socialised children and irresponsible, workless and crime-prone adult males

Value consensus: The set of norms and values around which there is (supposedly) broad agreement in society; includes views on history, religion, morality, lifestyle and wealth

Values: powerful ideas shared by people in a culture about what is right and desirable and what is shameful or wrong; often expressed in behaviour as **norms**

Western culture: the culture of the UK, European countries, North America and Australia, that emerged out of the shared experience of Christianity, the Industrial Revolution and the development of democracy; an important part of **Global Culture**; responsible for Capitalism

White collar crime: crime carried out by powerful people in the course of doing their respectable jobs; includes embezzling money, tax fraud, breaking health & safety regulations and environmental pollution.

Working class: The majority group in society that is systematically excluded from access to wealth and power; controlled by **ideology** and the threat of force by the **ruling class**; Marx terms the working class 'the proletariat.'

ABOUT THE AUTHOR

Jonathan Rowe is a teacher of Religious Studies, Psychology and Sociology at Spalding Grammar School and he creates and maintains **www.psychologywizard.net** and the **www.philosophydungeon.weebly.com** site for Edexcel A-Level Religious Studies. He has worked as an examiner for various Exam Boards but is not affiliated with OCR. This series of books grew out of the resources he created for his students. Jonathan also writes novels and creates resources for his hobby of fantasy wargaming. He likes warm beer and smooth jazz.

Printed in Great Britain
by Amazon

43303948R00097